"*The Spark and the Grind* is a battle cry for any artist who is looking to take the next actionable steps in building your creativity into a thriving band, brand, or business."

—Switchfoot, alternative rock band

"Reading this book is an investment in yourself. As a longtime 'grinder,' always willing to work hard but not always on the right things, I was inspired by Erik's practical advice. Harnessing creativity requires creative thinking, and this book shows you exactly how to do it."

**—Chris Guillebeau, author of *Born for This*
and *The $100 Startup***

"To read this book is to love it—and then to love your life and work in a new way. It's about passion, purpose, and constant creation in everything we do. It's nothing short of an exuberant, inspirational, and deeply practical guide to making the most of our days."

**—Tom Morris, author of *If Aristotle Ran General Motors*
and *The Oasis Within***

"Erik Wahl's book provides a deeper understanding of our world and our minds. It deconstructs the process and secrets of cultural, science, and business leaders, illuminating not just the why of their success, but also the how, for the rest of us."

—Annie Duke, world champion poker player

"Sometimes our biggest differentiating factor is the grind of our hustle. Sometimes it's the spark of our brilliant ideas. Always, it's the combination of both. There's no one better to learn from about this topic than Erik, who lives and breathes *The Spark and the Grind*."

—Amy Jo Martin, author of *Renegades Write the Rules*

"Whether or not you consider yourself to be a creative person, you'll be fascinated by *The Spark and the Grind*. Using these two words, Erik Wahl analyzes the creative process while teaching us about ourselves. Read this book and learn how to get your creative juices flowing!"

—**Ken Blanchard, coauthor of *The New One Minute Manager*® and *Collaboration Begins with You***

THE SPARK AND THE GRIND

THE
SPARK
and the
GRIND

IGNITE THE POWER OF
DISCIPLINED CREATIVITY

erik wahl

PORTFOLIO / PENGUIN

An imprint of Penguin Random House LLC
375 Hudson Street
New York, New York 10014
penguin.com

Most Portfolio books are available at a discount when purchased in quantity for sales promotions or corporate use. Special editions, which include personalized covers, excerpts, and corporate imprints, can be created when purchased in large quantities. For more information, please call (212) 572-2232 or e-mail specialmarkets@penguinrandomhouse.com. Your local bookstore can also assist with discounted bulk purchases using the Penguin Random House corporate Business-to-Business program. For assistance in locating a participating retailer, e-mail B2B@penguinrandomhouse.com.

ISBN: 9780399564208 (hardcover)
ISBN: 9780399564222 (ebook)

Printed in the United States of America
3   5   7   9   10   8   6   4   2

Book design by Daniel Lagin

*This book, my love, and my life, are dedicated to my wife, Tasha.
Without you there is no me. You are the primary promoter
and protector of my relationship with creativity.*

*This book is a reflection of our work together: the spark that
gives meaning, and the grind that gives the passion to the strength
of our marriage and the success of our business.*

CONTENTS

0

CREATIVITY IS A COMPLICATED FRIEND

CREATIVITY IS A COMPLICATED FRIEND.

But not at first.

When you and creativity initially met, you were young and the friendship was fast and easy. Wherever you went, creativity went, too. It never argued about the rules or who went first or whether an idea was relevant. And no matter how many times the two of you crashed and burned, creativity dusted itself off and was ready for more.

Then, sometime in middle school or high school, your relationship with creativity started to change. It's hard to say whose fault it was, but suffice it to say you two began growing up and growing apart.

You sought creativity's input less and less. Schoolwork and homework didn't require its companionship, and while you remembered fondly those carefree hours in the backyard—maybe even missed them now and then—there wasn't time for that anymore. Getting older meant your time was occupied by more "mature" activities. Your days of role-playing and fort building were replaced by studying and socializing and sports. Although creativity was welcome when it showed up, its youthful exuberance made things a little awkward. It was like a goofy younger sibling who wants to join but doesn't really fit in.

Creativity tagged along for a little while but eventually it just stopped showing up. You understood; it was an amicable separation, after all. You and creativity had simply grown apart. You didn't have the chemistry you once did.

One day, a few years later—probably when you set out to write your college entrance essay—you realized you could use creativity's input again. You called it up and asked it to coffee . . . but when you two sat down, creativity was cold. The relationship had become complicated—a connection that required work. Getting anything out of creativity was like pulling teeth. But with the help of a venti latte and a cinnamon scone, you got through the ordeal. Your entrance essay written, you said good-bye and parted ways again.

You went to college. You got a job. Maybe you got married and had some great kids. Now here you are. How many years has it been since you were close to creativity? Even as you reflect on how long it's been, you—like everyone else—hear creativity's name frequently. It's become a celebrity! Countless articles and books are written about it. Seminars praise its power. Gurus promise to reveal its secrets. Studies prove its indispensability. Everyone wants to know creativity again. Everyone wants a piece—to touch its cloak, to kiss its ring, to kneel at its altar.

What is it about creativity that draws us in? If we grasp it, understand it, embody it, we believe it can give us a new start. A first step. A cutting edge. A breath of fresh air. A breakthrough. Originality. Freedom.

Our desire for creativity is one of the most transcendent desires of our lives—if not *the* most. That's because our desire for creativity is ultimately a longing for more meaning, and more meaning breathes more life into our days. When our creations are an unobstructed outflow of our purest thoughts, beliefs, and convictions, our doing is in step with our being.

I'm not a vaunted sociologist, but I don't believe it takes a PhD to see that events over the past two decades—from 9/11 to the Great Recession to the rapid emergence of social media and the persistence of terrorism—have led to a recalibration of both personal and corporate values. Sure, the ability to BS ourselves and others will always remain. But the state of our world has prompted us to consider more deeply why we are doing what we are doing and where we are going. The beauty is that we live in an age where quick change is more possible than it's ever been. If we don't like why we are doing what we're doing or where we are heading, we have instant access to infinite resources that can help us alter our pace, direction, or trajectory. And we believe that creativity will get us to a better place, faster.

Whether or not you've experienced the spoils of creativity in your own life, we have all observed that a tight bond with creativity forges freedom and opportunity quite unlike anything else. Whether or not we understand it, we often desire it in the areas of our lives that matter most. We especially desire it in the areas where we sense we are either underperforming or off track.

This attraction is much bigger and broader than a desire to be a better artist in the traditional sense of the word. It's not just the authors, fashionistas, and interior designers looking for an in with creativity. All of us are looking for communion with creativity, including:

- Parents wanting to shape rambunctious offspring into thriving adults.
- Coaches scrapping for the secret sauce to inspire this year's team.
- Managers searching for the keys to engaging a new generation.
- Investors foraging for the next Spotify.
- Entrepreneurs aiming to become the next Elon Musk.
- Executives crafting the ideal culture.
- Lovers longing to last.

Creativity is a scorching-hot commodity. We are paying for it in historically large sums. And yet the investment isn't paying off as we'd expect.

On the corporate level, efforts to court creativity translate to serious money. According to "2015 Global Innovation 1000," a report produced by PricewaterhouseCoopers's consulting team Strategy& that details how much the top thousand public companies spend on innovation each year, total spending "increased 5.1% to $680 billion" in 2015. The top five companies leading the way were:

1. Volkswagen, at $15.3 billion or 5.7 percent of revenue
2. Samsung, at $14.1 billion or 7.2 percent of revenue
3. Intel, at $11.5 billion or 20.6 percent of revenue
4. Microsoft, at $11.4 billion or 13.1 percent of revenue
5. Roche (a biopharmaceutical company), at $10.8 billion or 20.8 percent of revenue

And yet, after conducting ten thousand analyses, the same study found no statistical relationship between increased innovation spending and:

- sales growth
- gross profit growth
- operating profit growth
- operating margin
- net profit growth
- net margin
- market cap growth
- and total shareholder return

In fact, the study's ten most innovative companies based on performance (led by Apple, Google, and Tesla) cumulatively outperformed the top ten spenders by nearly 10 percent—a trend that has held true for the last six years. Clearly, there is a tangible difference between treating creativity like a health supplement and treating it like the ecosystem in which your company breathes and operates. While casual dress codes, company retreats, and brand renovations can be effective additives in the body of a highly creative ecosystem, they are merely antacids in an organization that does not breathe creativity.

If you're not in the corporate world or otherwise affected by corporate performance, you're not out of the woods either. If you're, say, a full-time parent or a high school teacher or a physician in private practice, I daresay the same ineffectiveness is true for your personal investments into creativity and innovation. Legitimate statistics for individual R&D spending are nonexistent, but how many creativity seminars (or YouTube videos) have left you feeling full of inspiration that faded within a couple of weeks (if not days) and never translated into any sustained difference in your work or home life? How many blogs, articles, and books on innovation have you read that felt like they lit a flame under you, burning hot only until your creativity chops were actually tested? Generally speaking, how have your investments into bettering your creativity worked out for you thus far? I hope much better than what most people experience, which is that the burning flame didn't amount to much more in reality than a flicker of hope that always burnt out—fodder for a great tweet, but not for sparking greater imagination or fresh improvements in your life.

If you're like most, you're left to wonder: How is it that creativity seems to ooze from some people's pores while others struggle to squeeze out a great idea once a year? Maybe once a lifetime?

The relationship between you and creativity today is complicated. Let's start there. It's not effortless like it was when you were young. You have changed. Creativity has changed. Life is different now. You did, in fact, grow apart. Traditional schooling and typical corporate protocol have taught you that creativity isn't as important as finding the correct answer or following the correct strategy (as if there is always just one). As a result, your relationship with creativity takes real work today. And that's where the relationship stalls—even ends—for many of us.

The common practical response to this realization is that you will work at being more creative only when you need to—like when your marriage is dry or your job is drying up or your customer needs something better. It's the whole "necessity is the mother of invention" thing. So like a lonely former lover, you swallow your pride and reach out for some attention from creativity when you're feeling needy.

The common cynical response to realizing that connecting with creativity is hard is the proclamation that being creative on a regular basis is unrealistic and, frankly, takes a certain kind of quirkiness that doesn't play in all settings. "Creativity wasn't handed out to everyone for a reason" is the message.

Having internalized this message, people settle, and the act of creativity is relegated to requiring: 1) a great need, or 2) an eccentric nature. It makes the kind of daily relationship with creativity you had as a child seem completely out of the question, unless you're willing to be desperate or odd. The truth, however, is that you can rekindle that relationship. You just have to understand how to do it as an adult, because the way it works has changed. Here's what I mean.

Your childhood experience with creativity was real. To start, you needed creativity to learn your first language and understand how to get by in the world outside your mother's womb. Your brain and body were focused on breathing in as much data as possible to try to understand as much as possible. You didn't know, or care to know, what data mattered and what data didn't. You possessed an unconscious trust that the important concepts would illuminate themselves to you in time. In the meantime, you attempted much, ventured into whatever caught your attention, and had fun while doing it. Most important, you learned. Rapidly, in fact. You also started becoming who you would grow up to be.

Creativity was your trusty travel partner then. You trusted the relationship, or perhaps it's more accurate to say your genetic makeup trusted it. The products of your trust in creativity didn't always come easy. Remember skinned knees, twisted ankles, and burned fingers? You just accepted that you didn't know what you needed to know. And you innately understood that if you stuck with creativity, you would learn.

The neuroscience associated with this is heady, but the gist is that from the minute you were born you already had all the neurons you needed for a lifetime of learning. But those brain cells weren't yet linked with the complex networks needed for more mature comprehension of the world around you. So in your earliest years, your brain cells sought out and formed thousands of connections each day. While some of that process was genetic, your experiences were the primary catalyst that initiated connections and told you what went where and did what, and who was who. As a three-year-old, you had twice as many neural connections as you do today. Why? As you grew older your brain sought to become more efficient.

From about ten years old until adulthood, trillions of connections in your brain were systematically eliminated. How? According to use. Those connections that were reinforced—your daily interactions with caregivers, the ways you found nourishment, the language you used to communicate, your understanding of your environment, certain character traits—were locked in. Those connections that were not reinforced were treated as unnecessary or inefficient data in your brain and were promptly relegated to your brain's version of a junk folder.

One of the primary connections that was not reinforced was your connection with creativity.

At five years old, you went to school and, if that school was like the great majority of schools in the Western world, by about fourth grade an invariable learning style and a static theory of success and failure was reinforced daily. Becoming a big girl or big boy meant you needed to begin breathing out the results of the data you breathed in. Not a dynamic or personal translation of that data or a natural, cumulative revelation of that data—no, you were required to breathe out your teachers' and your books' translation of that data. Give the "right" answers, in other words. Suddenly, the hallmarks of your relationship with creativity—unbridled curiosity, unlimited fantasy, and discovery through trial and error—were no longer reinforced. Before long, your brain shed its inherent, trustworthy connection with creativity.

This was growing up under the governance of traditional education: you breathed in the data that your teachers and books said you should breathe in, and you breathed out their translation of that data, which were the only answers you needed to know in order to move on to the next grade with your friends, and ultimately grow into a smart, hardworking grown-up who could do anything you wanted to do.

Unless, of course, you wanted to be someone or do something that required a lot of imagination or originality.

Turns out that's most of us. It's definitely you. In that case, you will need to unlearn how you were taught to think and learn.

More specifically, you'll need to figure out how to know and trust creativity again, as an adult, which starts with a clear understanding of what creativity really is. Turns out it has grown up, too.

———

Here's the good news: you can learn to trust creativity again. On a daily basis. As a result, you can learn to churn out more vibrant, imaginative results from your efforts.

Here's the bad news: that has nothing to do with dressing more casually or sipping more coffee or working in the corporate equivalent of a McDonald's playhouse. At best, those efforts might put you in the mood to be more creative, but they'll never generate more creative results on a regular basis.

Trusting and utilizing creativity as an adult involves simultaneously embracing two concepts that, in your mind right now, probably sit on two different planets. And yet these two concepts are the two sides of the same coin we call creativity. They also make up the title of this book:

The Spark.

The Grind.

The Spark

The spark is what we traditionally think of as the start of creativity—an initial illumination. It denotes the most basic understanding, the lowest common denominator of creative production. It's what we first hope for when we're looking for that creative edge, that game-changing idea, that fresh catalyst for progress. We commonly refer to it as a lightbulb moment or a bolt of lightning. The inference is that it comes suddenly, unexpectedly.

Although I get the metaphors, they're actually poor ones. The truth is that the best ideas (and subsequent outcomes) are always the result of personal effort, and creative results can come to be expected. This is why the spark is a better symbol for creative insight.

The National Geographic Channel TV show *Naked and Afraid* provides a good, and quite unforgettable, example of what I mean by the spark. It's a reality survival show in which a male and female contestant, who've never met, are dropped off in some remote and unusually dangerous locale, sans clothes, and try to survive for twenty-one days on only the food, water, and shelter they find in the wild. In almost every episode, we're shown a scene in which the contestants are trying to start a fire. Next to locating water, starting a fire is arguably the most important key to their survival. Without fire they can't boil the impurities out of water to make it drinkable, they can't cook any meat they kill, and they can't warm themselves at night.

All they need is one spark to create an ember that ignites their nest of kindling. If and when they finally produce it, a celebration ensues, and life can go on.

I've watched contestants labor for hours into the night to light a fire using a primitive hand-drill or bow-drill method.

I've also watched contestants generate that ember in a matter of minutes. Either way, the result—that life-giving fire—was predicated on at least some personal effort rather than some paranormal (or meteorological) force.

Generating creativity is, at the outset, like that. It takes a personal effort to make the initial spark—whether it is an idea, strategy, or product—that you hope will ignite your relationship or company or campaign. Thomas Edison once locked himself and five coworkers in his lab, where they labored for sixty hours without sleep to finish a working printing machine. That's more work than a Starbucks espresso and one album on your noise-canceling headphones.

You have to be careful how you perceive the spark. History loves to trivialize creative output, as it has Isaac Newton's work on gravity with the popular anecdote that it hadn't come to him until that old apple fell on his head. Then, suddenly, the spark glowed to life. The truth is that many Newton biographers—Pulitzer Prize–finalist James Gleick being one of them—aren't convinced the falling apple incident ever happened. There is no mention of it in his own writings. Whether or not it's true doesn't matter, though, because what we do know is that discovering gravity was no serendipitous moment. Newton ignited many sparks for many years. He built a working model of a windmill at age eleven. He discovered the color spectrum and calculus when he was in his midtwenties. Approximately twenty years later, in his midforties, he discovered and published his findings on the three laws of motion, from which all modern physics is derived. And then came gravity.

If Newton had stopped with his first spark, he would be known today—if he was at all—as the boy who built a working model of a windmill at age eleven. But he didn't stop there. Isaac Newton was driven to understand how things worked. He immersed himself in all facets of math and science. When the plague hit Cambridge University and a college-aged Newton was forced to return home to the English countryside, he created a small study in his parents' home. In this study, he pulled out a blank thousand-page journal that he named his Waste Book and then, according to biographer James Gleick: "He began filling it with reading notes [which] mutated seamlessly into original research. He set himself problems; considered them obsessively; calculated answers, and asked new questions. He pushed past the frontier of knowledge (though he did not know this). . . . Solitary and almost incommunicado, he became the world's paramount mathematician." Newton filled his Waste Book with more than one million words before he made concrete discoveries. Before he was a famous mathematician, before he understood gravity, Newton would have been called neither an innovator nor a creative. If anything, he would have been called a hard worker who was very curious. Fortunately, it was in this context—diligently stoking the sparks of his imagination—that the results of his efforts caught fire.

Which brings us to the other side of the coin.

The Grind

The grind is the work of creativity.

This is the first truth you have to understand about creative endeavors: the spark comes to life at the expense of the grind. You will always run into problems when your efforts stop at the initial spark because rarely is the first spark the hottest, most potent spark. This was clearly true with Edison, who went on to win more than a thousand patents—including the iconic lightbulb—by working eighteen-hour days most of his life and famously finding "10,000 ways that won't work."

Creativity is no longer natural or free like it was when you were a young child. As an adult, it takes you more work to ignite a single spark than most people want to admit. And you have the critical eyes of others or the accountability of a marketplace surrounding you. But there's an important caveat. And this is the second truth you have to understand about creativity: it's a numbers game.

One spark alone is rarely enough. The more you grind at any given endeavor, the more you learn: about the process, about the outcomes, and about yourself. Your increased competence increases the likelihood of generating more sparks—or a bigger spark than the original. The more and bigger sparks you generate, the more likely you are to ignite an extraordinary blaze.

Ongoing, original creativity requires the spark and the grind: the initial flicker of hope and the work to stoke it into something that changes the game. Always both, never just one. In the coming pages, we will dive into the intricacies of both, the best practices as well as the pitfalls to avoid. For now, let's make sure we're clear on why both are necessary.

The Spark Without the Grind

The spark without the grind is the land of dreamers: coffeehouses across America, exposed-beamed scored-cement office buildings. Such places are the temples of creativity seekers and people who might call themselves creatives. But the final measure of creativity, innovation, or revolution is neither ideas nor dreams. It's whether those sparks grow into something that matters. Martin Luther King Jr. had a dream. He went about stoking it into a blaze that cleansed our nation. Would the spark have ignited as it did if King had only given a single speech?

People who chase the spark but don't embrace the grind are into igniting big ideas but not fanning them into a tangible blaze. Others might call them "idea people" and "visioneers," but the wake of their finished work reveals the truth. I call them Igniters. They are tempted to enjoy the reputation of creativity—the iPad commercial version—but not the reality of creativity.

Being an Igniter is harmless (sort of) if your objective is creating a provocative social media profile or garnering attention at a dinner party. But being an Igniter is frustrating and insufficient if you're trying to make fresh progress. Dreamers and visionaries are wholly necessary in our world; but left alone, the ideas they ignite would remain undeveloped.

All is not lost, however. There is hope for the Igniters of the world.

The Grind Without the Spark

The grind without the spark is what we feel when we say work is a grind. It is work for the sake of working, spinning your wheels, continual effort without meaningful progress. In other words, what makes the grind more grindlike is an absence of sparks, an absence of freshness or originality. The grind's effect on us is ultimately a matter of how it is used and what it produces.

It's not enough to grind only for money or position or prominence. These results have diminishing returns. You burn out. You fail and can't find the will to grind again. The results that grow your strength and willingness to keep grinding—that give meaning to the grind—are visceral. Meaning lives inside us. But it is manifest through the act of creation. When your work does not bring pieces of yourself into being, it quickly becomes a maddening grind. When your work does manifest pieces of you, the hours you must put in rarely matter.

Those who embrace the grind but not the spark, I call Grinders.

They wholly embrace labels that denote a strong work ethic; they gravitate to descriptions like "disciplined" and "driven" (because they sound a lot sexier than "cog" or "workaholic"). Hard work plays a critical role in anything, obviously. The reality, however, is that no one likes grinding for something that doesn't matter to them personally. If you're a Grinder, you know this is true whether or not you're willing to admit it (something that took me nearly a decade to do). It's exhausting to fake and yet millions do every day. Four thousand years ago, King Solomon wisely noted that because the traditional fruits of our labor—fame, possessions, titles—are inevitably meaningless; the best approach to life is to eat, drink, and grind at something that brings us joy (my paraphrase). In other words, the only grind that matters is the one that illuminates and fans the sparks inside us.

If you're a Grinder, it's time to open up and get real about why you grind. If you're willing to do this, there's hope for you, too.

"We are born makers," writes Brené Brown, "and creativity is the ultimate act of integration—it is how we fold our experiences into our being." To be more creative more often—to be the maker you were born to be—you must learn to chase the spark and embrace the grind, not at the expense of each other but in concert with one another. This dualistic approach is what separates those who create constantly from those who struggle to create even when it matters most.

Before we get into the meat of what it takes to chase the spark and embrace the grind, it's good for all of us to remember that light-bulbs, iPods, and theories of gravity throughout history were never the result of the first spark. In the pages that come, we will dig into the original spark and ongoing grind behind some iconic creations, as well as the life-changing innovations of regular people like you and me. But to begin, let's be clear on one thing: your ideas, efforts, and creations rarely fall short because you aren't intrinsically creative enough. They fall short because you either fail to grind your sparks, or you fail to spark your grind. When you learn to do both, then you will know how to start a blaze.

In this book, we'll explore what it really takes to be creative on a regular basis. I use the term "really takes" from a place of personal conviction. Because here's my first confession: before I was an art-ist, before I was an author, before I figured out how to know and trust creativity, I was, for most of my life, a card-carrying corporate Grinder.

Yes, really.

I treated creativity like a sunset. I believed if I showed up at the right place and time, I had only to wait for it to appear like the glo-rious orange and pink hues of an evening sky. I could then bask in its glow, inhale its shot of inspiration, before it faded away. I even convinced myself that certain locations gave me better access to it, a better view, if you will, with a chance to capitalize on creativity a little longer.

The beach ten miles from my house.

Poolside in my backyard.

The empty foothills east of my home.

Peet's Coffee & Tea down the road.

These were the places where I believed the magic embers lay waiting to be stoked. Whenever I needed them, I'd go there, poke around, and ignite a game-changing idea for my family, my career, or my business.

Then I'd pack up my Moleskine and get back to work.

Creativity was something I pursued only when I needed it. Aside from these fleeting, utilitarian moments of ignition, my days were governed by the grind. I grabbed hold of each morning with a vice-grip and pounded the subsequent hours into whatever shape I needed them to be.

It felt good. Strong. Productive. My career goals were singular and my strategy was focused: work as hard as possible to acquire as much net worth as possible in the shortest amount of time possible. The strategy worked well for eight years—until the economy began to show some cracks . . . and then imploded.

The dot-com boom busted at the turn of the century and my financial security went with it. I was in sales and suddenly companies that had been eager to pay for my company's service were now holding on to their discretionary income.

What do you do when your customers stop spending money? I did what most do. I dialed up creativity in hopes of igniting that spark that would keep me rolling, in hopes of finding an idea that would differentiate me from those who were struggling, and that would boost my business so it wouldn't fail. I needed to find a way to keep selling in a marketplace that had suddenly stopped spending.

I dialed up creativity . . . and redialed . . . and redialed again. I tried the beach, the café, the mountains, the pub, the church, and the gym. As they say, I left no stone unturned to find some spark, just one good idea that could save my business and career.

What had worked for me in the past—grinding more hours—worked only now and then. I'd close a deal and think, *This is it! I'm on my way back!* Then I wouldn't close anything for weeks. Then weeks turned into months. I worked more and more. Nothing seemed to stop the slide. I didn't know what I needed, and I certainly didn't know where to find it when I needed it most.

At the beginning of 2002, I accepted the inevitable and resigned before I was penniless. Even then, my wife, Tasha, and I didn't have enough to last for long, a few months at best, and it wasn't just ourselves we were supporting—we had three young boys to feed.

My career was gone. My financial security erased. Worst of all, my pride in being a proficient businessman was swirling down the toilet. I had so closely associated my net worth with my self-worth that when one started evaporating, so did the other. I began emotionally spiraling. It made me physically nauseated to think of my losses. I felt like shit. I kept asking, *How could this happen?* I'd never once been lazy. Never once cut corners. Never once missed a deadline—hell, I'd been early most of the time. Always did right by my clients. How, then? And why?

Though I didn't know it yet, the answer to my questions centered around my relationship—or lack thereof—with creativity. When I needed a spark to save my livelihood, I couldn't find one. My hard-ass work had succeeded for so long that it was truly alarming when I could not resurrect my career by grinding even harder. I certainly could have found solace in many unhealthy addictions—fortunately, I stumbled onto an unlikely possibility instead. In retrospect, I needed the grind to fail me before I ever would have considered looking for new sources of hope.

In the ashes of my loss, desperate and free from my old expectations, I was introduced anew to creativity. The reintroduction eventually changed everything—my career, my outlook, my marriage, my skills, my future. In truth, knowing the real creativity introduced me to my whole self and prompted me to become all I was made to be. I was given a new lens through which to view the world.

It started when, in my desperation to uncover a new career path, I dove into the local artist community in Southern California. I wasn't looking for financial advice. I was looking for sparks and I figured artists had a lot of them. I befriended these people and talked shop with them. I enjoyed their world and began to associate myself with it. But the more time I spent with them, the more I learned, to my surprise, that the majority were starving despite being very talented. Most were not taking in enough money to pay their monthly bills, and because their art was not being recognized, they had started to become detached and highly opinionated, believing that the world just didn't "get" them. Many descended into self-absorption and even depression. They worked other jobs to make ends meet or they scraped by.

Because I'd just come from the corporate world, I also noticed many of these same people held a subtle apathy toward personal discipline. They created when the spirit moved them, not with any regularity, and they were mostly uninterested in basic business strategies, like marketing and distribution and sales, to elevate their careers. They expected making good art to naturally evolve into making good money. They believed buyers would eventually notice them. Trouble was, as far as I could tell, they almost never did.

That was my first hint that there was a fundamental reality about progress—from the first step to sustaining improvement and avoiding collapse—that I had been missing. If discipline and integrity weren't enough to keep a career or business alive, and ideas and talent weren't enough to guarantee a person would thrive, then what was?

I'll tell you the full story a bit later, but for now I'll just say that when the lights went on for me a few weeks later, I realized I was onto something big, an idea that I'd never read in any business or personal growth book before. The essence is this: all progress rises and falls on our relationship with creativity. And because that's true, the key to constant improvement—whether it's renovation, transformation, or resurrection that's needed—is understanding how to stay connected to creativity.

This paradigm is like nothing I'd considered before losing my career. But I am tangible testimony to its effectiveness.

Today I am doing what I was made to do. Most people who've met me in the last fourteen years call me a speed painter or an artist, but those are just job descriptions. Yes, I paint large portraits in three minutes from a stage. In doing so I often look like the definition of an Igniter, full of ideas and inspiration. But pulling off a hundred keynote performances around the world each year for more than a decade requires more than ideas and inspiration. To get where I am, and to keep improving, I've embarked on a constant, strategic grind. To this day I am still more naturally a Grinder than an Igniter. But crucially, I've learned how to be both every day, and each time I step onto a stage. I've learned how to keep igniting ideas and keep grinding them out.

As I've grown and evolved as an artist, a speaker, a business owner, and a consultant, I've picked up a few lessons along the way. But because I'm a deconstructor by nature, I haven't learned dozens and dozens of trendy tips about creativity. I've learned a few timeless truths. I'm far more interested in what has always worked—regardless of era, fashion, and cultural context—than in the latest hack that works today but may be cliché tomorrow. In the last decade and a half, I've asked a lot more "whys" about being creative than "whats": I've constantly asked why creativity is a constant stream in some people and not in others. Asking that question has led me to a much shorter list of "whats" and "hows" surrounding constant creativity— seven, to be precise.

While I'll never claim to own an exhaustive list of keys (because I'm always learning and honing), the pages that follow lay out what I believe—through study, experience, and personal application— are the seven practices you must embed not just into your daily routine but also into your mind-set and spirit if you want to be creative on a regular basis in any area of your life.

In laying these out for you, my deepest hope is not only that your daily responsibilities will immediately be injected with a new sense of vibrancy and meaning; it is also that the trajectory of your life and career and business will expand and become more colorful and potent with possibilities that once seemed impossible, unrealistic, or out of character. I want you to enter into an ever-passionate, ever-productive relationship with creativity that inspires and continues to change you for the rest of your life.

1

TRUST THE PROCESS

The traveller sees what he sees; the tripper sees what he has come to see.

—**G. K. Chesterton**

IT WASN'T UNTIL THE SUCCESSFUL CAREER I HAD BUILT on grinding crumbled away that my view of creativity changed. Looking at my life George Bailey–style, I saw a really hardworking guy who didn't know what he'd been missing. I saw a dedicated husband and a father to three young boys who loved his family and meant well, but who was seriously limited by a philosophy that convinced him that grinding was the lone god of provision and prosperity. I also saw a guy who hadn't so much been fooled by that notion as a guy who'd been too stubborn to see the whole truth.

When being the hardest worker fell short, either I had to embrace Einstein's definition of insanity, expecting better results from the same approach, or I had to discover a better approach and hope for better results, which is the only sane way I knew.

I was searching for that better way when I finally came to see the whole picture. This, in summary, is what I learned: creativity improves everything from how you think to how you love to how you work, but not until you understand that being diligent is not enough, nor is having great ideas. Finding a way to embody both is the only way to tap the full potential of your creative power—and yes, it is in you to be tapped. That starts when you acknowledge your current tendency.

So, which are you today?

A Grinder like I was?

Or an Igniter?

Don't be heroic with your answer. Be real. Own who you've been to this point. Because your tendency is already a good thing.

The world needs people who enjoy swimming in ideas until they discover a great one. The world also needs doers who have a gift for activation, aka, "getting shit done." In fact, it makes for a great pairing when an Igniter and a Grinder (or a group made up of equal parts) work together, relying on one another's strengths to create something great. But the most potent individual creators in any industry or environment have learned how to be both. They've learned how to spark their grind and they've learned how to grind their sparks. As a result, they not only make things happen, they make great things.

While great creators possess proficient ability in both activities, it is most accurate to say that they intuitively know when to step back and swim with the sparks, and when to lean in and grind out a single idea. When to expand and think, and when to contract and do. This back and forth happens so fluidly that the best creators never think, *Now it's time to pause and think,* or *Now it's time to lean in and work.* While they grind out a single idea, they remain aware that more promising ideas might appear or a more promising path might evolve from the original idea. While considering a host of ideas, they remain primed to jump after a brilliant one and work it out.

For this reason, their application of creativity looks as natural as breathing. They appear to bleed creative things. What's really occurring is that they are seamlessly exhaling to ignite and inhaling to grind. In and out they continue. Creativity is their oxygen. Along the way, creation happens; products come alive as they go. This is why the Italian filmmaker Federico Fellini explained, "Making movies is like making love. . . . that's when I'm most fully alive. It's my most virile moment."

Do you share his feelings?

You can.

Great creators embrace a discipline of thinking and a discipline of doing. In embracing both disciplines, these once-voluntary and independent patterns become involuntary and interdependent. The disciplines evolve from something that feels like a regimen to something that feels like a lifestyle. From activities that feel like burdens to activities that feel like nourishment.

Ernest Hemingway is often caricatured as a virile, globe-trotting hedonist who loved wine and women and was preoccupied with violent activities like boxing, bullfighting, and big-game hunting. The truth is that he was quite volitional in all he did. The approach was largely the legacy of his father, Clarence Edmonds Hemingway, a midwestern physician who despised loafing and believed in constant self-improvement, going so far as to insist his six children "adopt a devoutly ethical approach to recreation."

Despite his father's stern and often gruff parenting style, Hemingway embraced a notion that even leisure activities like traveling, eating, and drinking should serve a purpose in his pursuits. He therefore approached each with an adventurous instinct and audacity that gave the appearance of constant intemperance. But as a writer, the belief translated into a vibrant, daring professionalism that made Hemingway world renowned before he turned thirty, and a Nobel and Pulitzer Prize winner before he died.

As Hemingway saw it, his life was all research—glorious and gory research—for his books. He lived as he wrote and he wrote as he lived. And although the end of his life was as tragic as his career was iconic, I'm guessing few would turn down a page from his epic adventures on the African plains, or on a moveable feast through the pubs of 1920s Paris, or on a twin-deck, liquor-stocked fishing vessel off the coast of 1950s Cuba.

Hemingway was a master of embracing the everyday highs and lows of life—relationships, responsibilities, and rigors—and mining every bit of beauty, energy, and emotion from them. To call such a man a hedonist is far from accurate. While he was certainly an admirer of beauty and pleasure, you'll see that he was too utilitarian about his experiences to be characterized in such fashion.

Hemingway had a process. He is best known for all the sparks he ignited—both the Nobel- and Pulitzer-worthy ones and the scraps more fitting for reality TV. But he was also a Grinder through and through. His creative process was never one without the other, and it was his ability to hold the spark and the grind in balance that led to his legendary success.

There's a widespread misconception that creativity and productivity rarely coexist in one person, unless you're from a rare breed, like Hemingway or Fellini or Madame Curie. Look at how most companies operate. We pay somebody to spend the day ideating and brainstorming and sipping espressos. And we pay somebody else to spend the day getting shit done. We have the espresso sippers from marketing, design, and PR over there in the industrial warehouse with scored cement floors and exposed beam ceilings. And we have the doers in sales, customer service, and fulfillment over there in the beige building with beige cubicles and beige walls. It's as if we have to choose one or the other, when the reality is that we don't—and shouldn't.

Unfortunately, the common compartmentalized thinking has ultimately led to an implicit disenchantment with the idea that an individual can be highly creative and highly productive on a daily basis. Corporate America usually treats sparking the grind and grinding the spark as divergent activities that can't be performed by the same person. My feet were planted firmly in this camp for a decade.

I didn't consider myself a "creative." I didn't see the need. I was a doer. Doing got results. And when I needed a new idea or better solution for something I was doing, I pressed pause and spent an impatient hour or two at the beach or the local Peet's. Then I got right back to work.

I thought I had the answer to igniting progress. I didn't. Constant creativity isn't playing pretend at a coffee shop when you need an idea, and then going back to "real" work. It's a fluid process that, with practice, allows you to intuitively grasp when to back off and ignite sparks, when to lean in and grind sparks out, and how to keep both options available at all times—because there are seasons when you have to do both simultaneously. Because I didn't understand any of this, my killer ability to grind wasn't enough to sustain eight years of promising progress.

While we all have some Igniter and Grinder in us, most of us rely on one approach to be successful, as I did. We're primarily thinkers. Or we're primarily doers. We traffic in ideas. Or we traffic in results. That's why one of the biggest creative strides you can make is to learn how to operate in both ways. Here's where that begins.

To grind your sparks and spark your grind . . .
TRUST THE PROCESS

You've probably heard the popular quote by the guy who cocreated Atari, the original Gen X home gaming system. His name is Nolan Bushnell, a talented entrepreneur now in his seventies who once said, "Everyone who has ever taken a shower has had a good idea. The thing that matters is what you do with that idea once you get out of the shower." He's also said, "Success does not follow ideas; success follows hard work."

Solid quotes, right? Grinders unite under this banner. But is he right?

Yes and no.

If you want to create anything at all, yes, you do in fact have to get out of the proverbial shower with your idea and do something more with it than fantasize about how successful it could be. Something more than spending the day at Starbucks. Something more than filling a whiteboard. Something more than buying the domain on GoDaddy or designing the logo with Illustrator.

Yes, Mr. Bushnell, "success follows hard work."

But it also requires ideas.

When this is forgotten, creative sparks can grow into flames and then die out before becoming a massive blaze.

With his Atari idea, Nolan Bushnell certainly got out of the shower and did something about it. Under his plucky grind, Atari became successful in the mid-1970s and he profited nicely. Leaning on the popularity of the video game *Pong,* and seeking more capital to expand, he sold Atari to Time Warner in 1976 for $28 million and bought his family a beautiful mansion. Bushnell remained at the helm of Atari for two years before he was ousted by the Warner board over differences in growth strategy. Under Warner's leadership, Atari went on to become America's fastest-growing company by 1982, reaching a peak of $1.3 billion in sales before crashing and being sold off in pieces less than two years later.

Maybe just bad luck? Corporate politics gone awry? Possibly.

After he was forced out at Atari, Mr. Bushnell turned his focus to a side gig he'd launched during Atari's first years called Chuck E. Cheese's Pizza Time Theatre. He'd originally created it as a distribution channel for his Atari arcade games. Now he had the time to give the idea more focus. He put in the work to expand the creation and then handed off the day-to-day reins in the early 1980s, using profits from the pizza restaurants to fund a couple of other sparks that captivated him, including a coin-operated game business he called Sente and an early attempt at computer animation he called Kadabra-scope. Unfortunately, the plan didn't succeed for long.

The Cheese was bleeding cash by 1983, which compelled Bushnell to sell off his other two interests. It wasn't enough. By 1984, the Chuck E. Cheese's Pizza Time Theatre filed for bankruptcy. From there, its debt was assumed by a competitor, who unified its own restaurants and brand under the Chuck E. Cheese moniker, which today has approximately five hundred locations. All was not lost for Bushnell, however, as the *Atlantic*'s Alexis Madrigal described in 2013 following an interview with the entrepreneur: "It got messy towards the end of Bushnell's involvement with Chuck E. Cheese in the mid-1980s. I don't want to get into the details, which are dizzyingly complex and contested. . . . In the end, Bushnell says that he cleared maybe $35 million."

Once again, another salute-worthy payday from an idea. But as Bushnell admits, in the same interview, "It wasn't bad, but it wasn't $200 million."

Let's pause there.

While Bushnell was nowhere near finished—even though tens

of millions would be more than enough for most of us to cash in our careers—this stage in his idea-filled career is ironic in retrospect.

As Mr. Bushnell famously says, ideas require doing the work. He cleared $60 million from grinding out just two of his original sparks. He was right about being a doer. But he was wrong about being a dreamer—and it cost him exponentially more than he made.

In the first two years of Bushnell's effort to erect the Atari empire—from 1972 to 1974—he hired two eccentric computer nerds by the names of Steve Jobs and Steve Wozniak to help him develop an Atari game called *Breakout*. About a year after their contract work was completed, the same two guys returned to Bushnell with an idea for an original home computer. Because they had used some parts borrowed from Atari to create their prototype, Jobs and Wozniak offered their design to Bushnell first. But Bushnell didn't see the value in their product. He was focused on grinding out the video game idea and continuing to fan that flame.

A year later, Jobs met with Bushnell again, alone this time, and asked him to invest in the home computer venture he and Wozniak were now calling Apple. Again, Bushnell passed, citing a desire to stay focused on the growing Atari brand. Years later, he confessed, Steve "asked me if I would put $50,000 in and he would give me a third of the company. I was so smart, I said no. It's kind of fun to think about that, when I'm not crying."

Atari sparked into a nice fire. But it was no Apple.

Chuck E. Cheese was a nice follow-up act to Atari. It more than doubled Bushnell's profits, which earned him more margin to create and chase more sparks. Furthermore, he became known as the creator of not one but two iconic Gen X products. As Madrigal puts it, "If you grew up in the 1980s, the same guy . . . is basically responsible for a good portion of your childhood longings."

But then again, the Cheese is no Pixar, which is what Bushnell's hasty sell-off, Kadabrascope, would become under its new owner, George Lucas.

Grinding the product—and grinding hard—made Nolan Bushnell a multimillionaire. Few would balk at being the creator of Atari and Chuck E. Cheese. But then again, who wouldn't trade Atari and Chuck E. Cheese for Apple and Pixar?

In terms of monetary value alone, Bushnell would be a billionaire today if he'd seen and seized only the opportunity Jobs presented to him. Is it such a huge stretch to think his name might then be as synonymous with Apple as Steve Jobs?

Yet even with the missed Apple opportunity, if Bushnell hadn't been so steadfast on saving Chuck E. Cheese in the early 1980s, who knows how much of Pixar (or Disney) he might own today. (Coincidentally, before his death, Jobs was also the single largest shareholder in Disney—of which Pixar became a subsidiary in 2006—with approximately $4.4 billion in stock).

While Jobs and Bushnell are different men with different skill sets and distinct personalities, for a decade they seemed to breathe the same oxygen in Silicon Valley. They simply treated the creative process differently.

To use G. K. Chesterton's line at the beginning of this chapter, Jobs was a "traveller." He saw what was there to see and that allowed his vision to continue evolving. Bushnell, on the other hand, was a tourist, what Chesterton called a "tripper." At least for a season. He saw what he came to see—the growth of the original idea.

To be fair, Nolan Bushnell is a very successful entrepreneur on at least two counts. First, he's known today as one of the fathers of the video game industry. Sparking an industry is a momentous achievement. Few come close. Second, he made a load of money fairly early. Again, a noteworthy, and extremely rare, achievement.

Nolan Bushnell produced two solid sparks that, according to his own advice, he worked hard to fan into two healthy, multimillion-dollar fires. That's more than most can say. But had he put more trust in the creative process by allowing himself to remain an Igniter, while manifesting the hardcore doer in him, the entire world would know his name today.

———

Fortunately, Nolan Bushnell is not merely a cautionary tale for those who want to be more formidable creators. He eventually learned to trust the fluid creative process that allowed him to continue dreaming while grinding out his ideas. This constant balance is key, and it is the only way you won't lose sight of bigger ideas while grinding, or lose opportunities while searching for a spark. More on that in a minute. First let's get clear on what it means to trust the process, in Bushnell's case, more than the product.

In any creative venture, whether you're crafting a new product, writing your autobiography, or launching a company, there are seasons of both clarity and confusion. Aha! moments, followed by What the hell?! moments. A hard charger has a tendency to push through the confusing moments with laser focus on the prize—the finished product or the goal that has already taken some tangible form in her mind, in a document, or on a whiteboard. Grinders rarely charge after something that doesn't have at least some clarity up front, an initial spark of insight, intuition, or understanding. That's because Grinders need a finish line. They are driven by achievement—by not only the elation of finishing, checking another item off the list, but also by the rewards of that achievement, whether they are economic, emotional, or hierarchical.

This nature to grind toward a goal is a beautiful thing. It's also necessary. But if it's all you do, grinding can cause you to be myopic and thus only a shell of your creative self. In other words, true Grinders rarely grind mindlessly but their laser focus can blind them to more creative possibilities.

In their excellent book, *Wired to Create,* which synthesizes the findings of decades of creativity research, authors Scott Barry Kaufman and Carolyn Gregoire cite "three main 'super-factors' of personality that are highly correlated with creativity: plasticity, divergence, and convergence." Plasticity, they explain, is all about possessing a deep-seated drive to explore. Divergence is about possessing a high degree of nonconformity and impulsivity. Convergence is about possessing an ability to be precise, conscientious, and persistent.

The third super-factor cited by Kaufman and Gregoire—convergence—is what Grinders own in spades. They are thorough and highly attentive to an end goal. They are doers who know how to get things done. This is critical when it comes to bearing out an idea. If you want to see what your idea looks like as a product, as soon as humanly possible hand it to a proven Grinder. Unfortunately, if the first idea doesn't pan out as well as you thought and you're looking for new ideas, Grinders aren't the best resource.

What Grinders tend to lack in their hard-line drive for the finish line are the other two super-factors Kaufman and Gregoire mention: plasticity and divergence. The sum of these two qualities is the genesis of originality, or what the authors call openness. While Grinders like Nolan Bushnell thrive in turning creative fiction into commercial reality, they often lag in their ability to see new ideas, especially during the drive to a finish line. To spot or summon fresh, even iconic ideas while grinding, you have to have some Igniter in you, too.

Grinders are driven to finish a journey; Igniters are driven to explore. "Dr. Kaufman's research," writes FiveThirtyEight lead science writer Christie Aschwanden in her *New York Times* review of *Wired to Create*, "has shown that openness to experience is more highly correlated to creative output than I.Q., divergent thinking or any other personality trait. This openness often yields a drive for exploration, which 'may be the single most important personal factor predicting creative achievement.'"

To drive this point home, in her review, Aschwanden cites Denise Shekerjian's 1990 book, *Uncommon Genius,* in which the author calls this openness to experience "staying loose, often without regard for practicality or efficiency." Igniters, in other words, don't mind the uncertainty of the unknown. They don't need a lane or a finish line—at least not right away—and it's this comfort with an undefined destination that often sparks the most original creations.

Of course, Igniters must do more than just explore, which is all that amateur Igniters do. They have to refine their discoveries and subsequently their creative trajectory. Still, explains Aschwanden, Kaufman and Gregoire's research makes an important point: "Those murky, ambiguous places . . . are quite often where the creative magic happens."

The mistake the Grinder makes with the creative process is that she worships the end product, the finish line, the reward that's in sight but just out of reach. The Grinder doesn't mind the murky ambiguity—in fact, it's probably more accurate to say she ignores it—because her eyes are 110 percent on the endgame, obstacles be damned. Get out of the Grinder's way. She's gonna finish that thing she set out to create if it kills her. Long hours? Par for the course. Late nights? Get her a Red Bull vodka and turn up the music. That vision she Sharpied out so clearly on the whiteboard will . . . be . . . reality. And it will increase revenue. And it will improve the company. It's not a matter of if. It's a matter of when. And the sooner is always the better.

Our friend the Grinder has embraced the grind to a demonstrative degree. She wears the long hours as a badge and, because she does, she must have the achievement to show for them. Great effort with no trophy eventually looks foolish, so she pushes herself past obstacles and earns the deserved prize. Trouble is, greater opportunity is often in those obstacles along the way. She just blew past a multimillion-dollar idea to earn the Marketer of the Month award in her company.

Most Grinders don't know what they miss because grinding produces rewards. Often, those rewards seem to prove their methodology. Nolan Bushnell is a case in point. Unfortunately, Grinders can fail to see that their methodology sets them up to trade the finish line for their finest work.

But Grinders aren't alone in their creative deficiency.

While the Grinder worships the end goal, the Igniter worships the early magic. He treats creativity like an evening sky in the South, full of fireflies. He snags one glowing bug after another and then releases them all and watches their little flames flicker up and away. The next evening, he's standing on that back porch again, scooping up those beautiful sparks and then setting them free.

Our friend the Igniter is often allergic to the grind. Or he mischaracterizes creativity as a wholly soft-skill endeavor that doesn't require grinding if the idea is good enough to stand on its own. While he has an uncanny ability to embrace the early mystery of the creative process, he often balks the moment the starry night gives way to the dawn, which is when the real work begins.

The Igniter who's unwilling to grind beyond the wonder—at times, even see beyond it—often ends up with doughy, half-baked ideas. He possesses the plasticity and divergence to discover good ideas anywhere, but he lacks the fervor to craft those discoveries into something tangible, let alone viable.

In *The Writing Life*, Annie Dillard describes the common debt great artists like Tolstoy and Gauguin express to other artists and the "range of materials" that fueled their ideas to become something tangible. "By contrast," she explains, "if you ask a twenty-one-year-old poet whose poetry he likes, he might say, unblushing, 'Nobody's.' In his youth . . . he himself likes only the role, the thought of himself in a hat."

This is the risk in being only an Igniter: you eventually come to enjoy the sight of yourself in a beret or beanie so much that you aren't eager to swap it for a hard hat. It's the gratification of a Hemingway lifestyle without the discipline to park your ass in front of a keyboard each day and write a thousand words.

In a recent *Psychology Today* article on the basis of aha! moments, author Bruce Grierson cites Louis Pasteur's famous line "Chance favors the prepared mind" as an affirmation of how life-changing ideas both come to us and alter our existence thereafter—but only as we pursue them. He explains that the creative process is never just the aha! or just the follow through. It's best described as a dynamic tension between the two.

"Research suggests," writes Grierson, "that thinking about a problem too methodically is often an impediment to solving it because we block potential solutions from floating into consciousness. . . . Incubating a conundrum isn't enough on its own. A puzzle will never be solvable if you don't have all the pieces." Grierson cites the work of University of California, Santa Barbara neuroscientist Jonathan Schooler, which shows that staying in grind mode too long often drives the solution away—an effect called cognitive inhibition.

But if we back off too soon, we miss finding all the needed puzzle pieces to complete the solution or craft the best creation.

Mark Beeman, a cognitive neuroscientist from Northwestern University, calls this a "back-and-forth between being very focused and not." If you're an Igniter, you're great at the "not" side of that continuum. You understand the importance of incubating an idea so, as Grierson puts it, you don't "crush the tender shoot of an insight" before it grows into something bigger. But there comes a time when the seed has been babied enough and you must begin farming it with daily labor. It won't grow on its own. If you stay in Igniter mode, you basically incubate your idea to death.

In contrast, the Grinder who's fiercely committed to the original idea—and fiercely blind to the additional seeds along the path of creation—often ends up with full-grown ideas that aren't refined. If you're only a Grinder, you possess all the necessary convergence to deliver but you lack the sense to step back along the way and either evolve your creations into more advanced versions or spot a better creation altogether.

This was not just Nolan Bushnell's story early in his career. It's the story of most true Grinders. Including me.

Before I learned to paint, I was a hardcore, blinder-wearing Grinder.

Work ethic was my first measuring stick. My father was an All-American athlete in two sports, a shortstop and a running back.

He taught me the value of training and straight-line focus. I embraced it.

When I joined the workforce in the mid-1990s, I made sure that I was the first to the office and the last to leave. I wouldn't be outdone. It would never be said of me that my effort came up short. I worked in what is known today as the thought-leader industry. I was a partner in a speakers' bureau, which back then was a major up-and-coming idea. My primary job was to introduce companies looking for a keynote speaker to unique people with fascinating experiences and big ideas.

I was up before dawn so that by six I could make calls to the East Coast. I did the little things that the other speakers' agents were not willing to do. I didn't just read the white paper on the people I represented; I got to know them personally. I sought to learn from their expertise so that I had a firsthand experience I could relay to the companies who might hire them. I carved out my niche, polished my brand of representation, and honed a highly successful business model.

For seven years I bought into the notion that grinding was the be-all and end-all. I had the proof. Work ethic equals success wasn't just a cliché or fluke in my experience. I had the success thing locked down. I was a rainmaker and the rain was pouring. For years it poured. Then something subtle began to happen inside me that I didn't see right away. I began measuring my worth by the trophies in my case—the uptick in income, the nicer toys, the bigger titles, the common bounty of the grind.

If I could buy a BMW instead of a Honda, it proved my

advancement. My first house wasn't enough. Soon I needed a bigger house. Trips up the coast to Laguna Beach or Santa Barbara were nice at first, but soon my wife and I began taking grander vacations. Then we talked about our vacations to our friends and acquaintances. It was proof that the long hours were working for me. I reveled in the growth of my bank account and stocks, and in experiences to share. If social media had been around I'd have looked like a young, jet-setting Richard Branson. You'd have seen my net worth expanding in photographic detail.

I monitored my stocks throughout the day; in the late 1990s this was like watching your favorite team on television run over their competition. The margin of victory increased by the minute and I couldn't look away.

But my philosophy wasn't evergreen. In the 1990s, the thought-leader niche hadn't yet fully bloomed before it suffered its first setback during the dot-com bust. As the market began to experience more volatility, businesses' discretionary funds were bottled up and fewer and fewer of them hired the keynote speakers I represented. I quickly realized I was neck deep in a young industry that sold a product that was widely seen as a luxury. The damage spread as my stocks began to plummet. Slowly, painfully, I watched every client and nearly every investment dollar disappear and the business I'd spent nearly a decade building flounder and eventually stagnate. I was pissed. I'd worked my ass off for years, constructing it brick by brick, painting the walls, laying the floors, and for what? I remember thinking I might as well have been a stoner. The result would have been the same and I'd have far better stories to tell.

It wasn't long before I was deeply in debt, with no prospect of future income. I felt furious and helpless, an unenviable mix. And I couldn't imagine going back to the same grind for another decade just to crawl back to where I'd been at twenty-nine.

The nights were poignant and difficult. I'd pace the moonlit house in circles, seething. I didn't want to start over. But I knew I had to. That knowledge was the worst part. What was I going to do with my life? I was young and still had a lot of time on Earth. I also had a mortgage, and Tasha and I were raising three children under six years old.

I needed a spark. Desperately needed one. In what business and with what tools, I didn't have a clue. I knew only how to grind the hell out of an idea until it produced a slice of heaven. The problem was that it worked for long enough that when it didn't, I had no prospects whatsoever. I'd long since turned my back on other opportunities. I'd been blind to all else but blazing the one path before me. When that was gone, I suddenly needed to come up with a new career out of thin air.

The anger I felt was largely the result of a lack of direction. I just wanted a definitive goal to grind toward. That was my comfort zone. I could control getting from A to B if I knew where B was.

What I didn't know is that another clear goal right then would have been the absolute worst thing for me. I'd have made the same mistake again. I'd have put the blinders back on and missed the lesson I needed to learn, which was to embrace the creative process. Learning this lesson is the primary reason I was able to evolve into the artist I am today. But to learn it, I needed to experience the beauty of the unknown in order to break free of always needing the known.

"Man is a creative animal," Dostoevsky asserted, "doomed to strive consciously toward a goal, engaged in full-time engineering."

Driving toward a goal is necessary. The goal fuels the kind of hard work that produces real progress. But when a killer work ethic is paired with a broadened perspective on what more that goal might become, your creativity comes alive. Sparks fly. And you become engaged in full-time engineering to capture and shape the best ones.

"I begin with an idea," explained Picasso, "and then it becomes something else." For Igniters, your lesson is in the becoming. Your ideas must be ground out for them to become something radiant. For Grinders, your lesson is in the beginning. You must allow your initial idea to be just that—a beginning—and as you grind you can begin to see it evolve into something else, something brighter, something you never could have whiteboarded at the outset.

We must all find ultimate value in the process of creation more than in any end product. A single spark is needed to start a fire. But don't celebrate too soon. Producing something is important. It's a worthy reward along the way. Enjoy it. But know it's only the beginning. Keep grinding—keep stoking—and keep watching for the swelling of the spark into something else, something hotter. The first spark is never the brightest one inside you.

Concurrently, not all sparks should stay alive. But those that should must evolve or expand. Igniters need to learn to grind ideas to evolve or expand them. Grinders need to unlearn their tendency to forget the fire for the prized ember.

———

A friend named Grant, who's written more than four dozen books, recently told me that he finally learned, three books into his career, that he could painstakingly determine up front what the book would be and then fight to keep that idea as the book for the next six to twelve months. Or he could get as much clarity up front as possible and then let go and write—not only taking the journey but taking in the journey like a traveler rather than a tripper, as G. K. Chesterton said.

To be more creative more often, you have to become a traveler who sets out in a direction to discover and evolve, not merely confirm. That's the creative process that has to be trusted. The more you grind into it and through it—murkiness, pain, and all—the more you learn to trust the sparks that arise as you go. They don't come one detached spark after another as if from some random universe you didn't know existed. The truth is that the rising sparks are really growing from the initial spark as it swells into a bigger and hotter flame. You might not recognize it as such. Certain new ideas and solutions may seem completely random because the newest sparks will be different in shape and size and heat. Sometimes they float off and start a new blaze. Sometimes they expand the original one. But they can always be attributed to a spark that came before them.

"Experimental innovators like [Chris] Rock, [Sergey] Brin and [Larry] Page, [Jeff] Bezos, and Beethoven don't analyze new ideas too much too soon, try to hit narrow targets on unknown horizons, or put their hopes into *one big bet*," writes author Peter Sims. "Instead of trying to develop elaborate plans to predict the success of their endeavors, they *do things to discover what they should do*."

By placing what Sims calls "little bets," we are able to identify more possibilities that ultimately swell to create greater outcomes. "At the core of this experimental approach," he explains, "little bets are concrete actions taken to discover, test, and develop ideas. . . . They begin as creative possibilities that get iterated and refined over time, and they are particularly valuable when trying to navigate amid uncertainty, create something new, or attend to open-ended problems . . . little bets help us learn about the factors that can't be understood beforehand."

The first spark of an idea sends a bit of euphoria through our veins; it's like a drug, and we can get hooked on that feeling. On one hand, we are meant to get hooked on that feeling. "Creation is a drug I can't do without," wrote the inimitable filmmaker Cecil B. DeMille. We are made to create; and witnessing something born from our beings is one of the greatest affirmations of our existence. Picasso claimed, "Creation is all." Coco Chanel confessed, "When I can no longer create anything, I'll be done for."

When we ignite a spark, our blood pulses gladly. Our bones rejoice. This is creativity's first reward.

But when our creative ventures end there, when we don't enter into what Nobel Prize–winner Isaac Bashevis Singer called the "chasm between . . . inner vision and its ultimate expression," we are no more than a junkie. Creativity is cheap heroin used only for a hit of euphoria. Left unchecked, this habit leaves Igniters like addicts whose lives are governed and even defined by the rising and falling of that feeling. But creativity is more than a feeling. More than ignition. More than a product.

It is as human as breathing and as crucial to our survival. Creating is our fundamental activity in life, proof that we are more than beings who are alive, proof that we are living and becoming. All we do is create, to some degree. The questions are: To what degree? And for what purpose?

"There is probably nothing more sublime than discontent transmuted into a work of art, a scientific discovery, and so on," said the seminal philosopher Eric Hoffer. This sublimity is creativity's ultimate reward. The distance between the blood-pulsing spark and that ultimate destination is the journey, the creative process.

Annie Dillard says the sensation of commencing the creative journey is like "peering from the bent tip of a grassblade, looking for a route." The eureka moment, the flame stretching higher, is a sensation of "unmerited grace . . . handed to you, but only if you look for it." In between, she says, creation is like wrestling an alligator with your bare hands.

The eureka of gravity didn't come from Newton whiteboarding the hypothesis of gravity and then grinding to prove it. The notion of gravity hadn't even crossed his mind in the beginning. The discovery came from Newton chasing a spark of fascination for engineering as a kid, which grew into a passion for math as a young man, which ignited his discovery of the color spectrum, a flame that was fanned into his discovery of calculus, and grew into his discovery of the laws of physics. The flames then burst into an inferno we know as gravity.

You could look at those sparks separately and make a case that being fascinated with engineering has little to do with discovering gravity. You could assert that kids everywhere are fascinated with things every day and they don't end up landing some world-changing discovery. You'd be right. You'd also be missing the point.

Initial sparks aren't that difficult to come by. To Nolan Bushnell's point, everybody has an idea in the shower. They aren't all game-changing ideas. Few are, really. Take Newton's windmill at eleven years old. Not every kid could do that—turn a visual of a windmill into a better version. But let's be honest—that's not particularly original or inventive. Resourceful kids everywhere are coming up with crazy new ways to do or make things. When Nikita Rafikov was eleven, he developed a way to light homes without electricity by embedding the bioluminescent green protein found in certain jellyfish into windows. Take that, Newton!

If anything, Newton's early sparks showed promise. He was very curious. Most important, he was willing to grind his curiosity through.

That's a key point. His curiosity never became static. As a result, the sparks continued to fly, and they created bigger and bigger flames. Being inventive—and especially being an original—takes work. There's no way around it. "A lot of people are so used to just seeing the outcome of work," said the late, great Michael Jackson. "They never see the side of the work you go through to produce the outcome." Yet this unseen locale is where the magic really happens.

In his fascinating book *How to Think like Leonardo da Vinci*, author Michael Gelb describes the seven "Da Vincian Principles" the world's preeminent Renaissance man lived by. Number one is what he calls Curiosità, which translates to curiosity or inquisitiveness. Gelb sums it up as "an insatiably curious approach to life and an unrelenting quest for continuous learning." He explains that in da Vinci's time, it was widely accepted that all knowledge was already known, and those who knew it—the "men of letters," as it were—were never questioned. Da Vinci didn't buy it. Gelb cites sixteenth-century biographer Giorgio Vasari, who, in *The Lives of the Artists,* points out that the young da Vinci questioned his mathematics teacher with such vigor and originality that "he raised continuous doubts and difficulties for the master who taught him, and often confounded him." This unrelenting inquisitiveness never slowed.

Da Vinci, writes Pulitzer Prize–winner Daniel Boorstin, was unlike Dante in that "he had no passion for a woman. Unlike Giotto, Dante, or Brunelleschi, he seemed to have had no civic loyalty. Nor devotion to church or Christ. He willingly accepted commissions from the Medici, the Sforzas, the Borgias . . . from the popes or their enemies." In other words, he remained open to discovery at every angle and even from those people, things, and disciplines in which the possibility of discovery didn't seem to exist.

Gelb concludes that "Leonardo's loyalty, devotion, and passion were directed, instead, to the pure quest for truth and beauty." Da Vinci roamed the hills where he lived to try to understand why seashells could be found on the mountaintops, and, in his own words, "Why the thunder lasts a longer time than that which causes it. . . . How the various circles of water form around the spot which has been struck by a stone." To learn anatomy, he dissected more than thirty human corpses. To learn sculpture, he studied living plants, animals, and humans.

While da Vinci remained open to learning from many great minds of his time, he never accepted their knowledge as his own. He tested it through experiments and personal experience and his own study of the conclusions. If he could not prove what he'd been told by the experts, he believed their knowledge to be false. This made him unpopular among many so-called authorities of his day, which he acknowledged by confidently pointing out that "experience . . . is the true mistress" and "the mother of all certainty."

Before you write off the examples of icons like Newton and da Vinci as rare breeds, be reminded that they grew up with far fewer resources than we have today. And before you write off the times in which they lived as chock full of opportunities to discover, remember that we didn't have smartphones just ten years ago, or Twitter, or Instagram. There is always more to learn, and more to be invented. The frontiers of creativity are endless. But to travel those frontiers you have to ascribe equal value to ideas and the grind that brings them to life.

Valuing ideas over hard work often leads to a lack of creations.

Valuing hard work over ideas often leads to anemic creations.

The secret to trusting the creative process lies in embracing the duality of creativity—that it is both a fresh idea and a fierce drive: not one or the other but both, at any time. Applying this to your day to day requires an ability to know which is needed during the course of creation. While you might automatically assume that ideation is the beginning of the creative process, this isn't always the case. Sometimes it's better to begin grinding the task at hand and let the sparks that fly reveal a bigger idea or a better path. The saying "It's easier to act your way into thinking than think your way into acting" comes into play here. Either way, there is no script for creativity. Sometimes the idea fuels the work. Sometimes the work fuels the idea. Your job is to begin and then remain open to toggling between the two activities, according to what is needed most—either more originality or more progress. Knowing when to toggle is largely based on your ability to remain fully present during the process. When you are present, you remain open to the learning possibilities in and around you.

———

In his book *The Art of Learning,* author and the subject of *Searching for Bobby Fischer* Josh Waitzkin describes the secret to becoming one of the greatest chess players in history. "My growth," he writes, "became defined by *barrierlessness.* Pure concentration didn't allow thoughts or false constructions to impede my awareness, and I observed clear connections between different life experiences through the common mode of consciousness by which they were perceived. As I cultivated openness to these connections, my life became flooded with intense learning experiences."

Waitzkin goes on to describe numerous instances through which his openness to learning reaped unexpected sparks. In one instance, he was sitting on a coastal cliff in Bermuda, watching the waves crash down, and suddenly the solution to a weeks-long chess conundrum came to him. He sparked a breakthrough in his Tai Chi mastery after studying a single chess position for eight hours. Shooting hoops in Manhattan helped him finally comprehend the Buddhist concept of fluidity.

"The world of actors and musicians is brimming with huge expectations, wild competitiveness, and a tiny window of realistic possibility," Waitzkin explains. "Two questions arise. First, what is the difference that allows some to fit into that narrow window to the top? And second, what is the point? . . . In my opinion, the answer to both questions lies in a well-thought-out approach that inspires resilience, the ability to make connections between diverse pursuits, and day-to-day enjoyment of the process."

Waitzkin sums up this approach by pointing to the Zen Buddhist concept called shoshin, which renowned Zen teacher Shunryu Suzuki first called "the beginner's mind."

The beginner's mind isn't difficult to understand. We've all been beginners at something, multiple times. But there's a big difference between a beginner who actively learns versus one who accepts lessons only passively. Shoshin refers to the former. The beginner who is eager to learn remains open to many possibilities and, as a result, learns not only more but in most cases more efficiently.

Why does the mind-set you take into the creative process matter? Because the only way you fan initial sparks into new and improved products is through a commitment to learning.

If we aren't eager and open to learn—if we don't find and trust a learning process—we will either miss better opportunities like a hyperfocused Grinder or we will shortchange the original opportunity like an unwitting Igniter.

How can we know these opportunities will arise? We can't. That's why creativity requires trust. But this trust never leaves us hollow. Even if we don't seize that game-changing idea along the way, even if we don't polish that viral product, we build our creative arsenal for the next opportunity. And we grow as creators with better senses about us.

"As a writer," asks author and screenwriter Steven Pressfield, "how do I know what a character will say? I don't. I have to trust . . . whatever comes through from the Muse, the unconscious, the Quantum Soup. I've tried patterning characters after real people, to help me get a feel for what they'll say. It never works. . . . My job is to find who each one is—and let that person come forward on his own."

Picasso explained the process this way. "The painter goes through states of fullness and evacuation. That is the whole secret of art. I go for a walk in the forest of Fontainebleau. I get 'green' indigestion. I must get rid of this sensation into a picture. Green rules it. A painter paints to unload himself of feelings and visions."

Trusting the creative process is like committing to an expedition in an uncharted land where beginning knowledge is limited and progress is governed by discoveries made, not distance covered. Your most important tools are observation and resourcefulness. There will be days when you can see where the path is heading and other days when the fog is so thick you can see little more than your hand in front of your face. On days when the horizon is visible you lean forward and stride resourcefully, with observation as your constant companion. On days when there is no horizon, you lean back and stroll observantly, with resourcefulness as your constant companion. While you might have certain expectations or hopes, there remains an implicit mystery about this journey. This is what drives you and every explorer before you: what might be.

When you have no clarity, you search fervently for the next spark, ready to grind after a promising one.

When you have a bead on clarity, you grind toward it, still aware of the sparks, not immune to them.

To be constantly creative, you must be both an Igniter and a Grinder—and you must understand when one role takes precedence over the other, without losing the other altogether. How? Practice. Your trust will grow as your creative prowess does. But don't fool yourself. This isn't that difficult.

If you lean toward being an Igniter, stop using brainstorming as a synonym for progress when you know it's more akin to procrastination.

If you lean toward being a Grinder, stop using focus as an excuse to ignore other opportunities around you.

If you can agree to be real with where you are right now, you can find creative freedom and reap the creative benefits sooner. You can learn to live out of a spark-and-grind paradigm in which you give both equal value. Although this sort of accurate judgment of your reality may not come naturally or confidently to you right now, don't let that keep you from seeking clarity. It's that important to know where you truly stand so you remain neither naïve nor myopic. Don't be afraid to ask people you trust to help you get real if need be. And don't be shy or embarrassed about this. I didn't see the fog my tendency had created. Had I seen it, or had someone I trusted shown it to me, circumstances could have rapidly swung in my favor.

———

In their groundbreaking book, *Art & Fear,* authors David Bayles and Ted Orland explain: "To all viewers but yourself, what matters is the product: the finished artwork. To you, and you alone, what matters is the process: the experience of shaping that artwork." This is likely why Michelangelo is said to have confessed that if we knew how much work went into his art, we probably wouldn't call it genius.

In 1990, psychologist Mihaly Csikszentmihalyi coined the term "flow" to describe the ideal state of creativity, in which a person's best intentions and instincts play out in perfect harmony, resulting in joy and optimal results. The more colloquial phrase for flow is "being in the zone." What ultimately happens when you are in the zone and experiencing flow is that you enjoy an activity for its own sake. As a result, you are able to suck every bit of beauty and joy and education from the experience. Csikszentmihalyi explains, "The key element of an optimal experience is that it is an end in itself. Even if initially undertaken for other reasons, the activity that consumes us becomes intrinsically rewarding." In the flow state, constant creators come alive and find their rhythm.

Csikszentmihalyi uses the term "autotelic," which is derived from two Greek words, *auto,* meaning "self," and *telos,* meaning "goal," to refer to a self-contained activity that is done for the reward of doing it. "Teaching children in order to turn them into good citizens is not autotelic, whereas teaching them because one enjoys interacting with children is," he writes. "What transpires in the two situations is ostensibly identical; what differs is that when the experience is autotelic, the person is paying attention to the activity for its own sake; when it is not, the attention is focused on its consequences."

The major benefit, says Csikszentmihalyi, is that an autotelic activity frees you up to sense all that is going on around you. Cue Waitzkin's "openness" here. You are able to live fully in the moment and don't miss the small details that enrich an experience. Imagine what this means for your creative endeavors.

What if you embarked on your next creative journey in an autotelic manner—whether it's writing a blog, teaching a class, or parenting a posse? What if you set out to simply enjoy being the best writer, teacher, or parent you can be?

When you embrace the creative process, you enter into an activity with the freedom to experience and learn from all it has to offer. That includes the thrill of seeing the finished product, but is not restricted to it. From that place you are able to seize the prime moments to lean in and grind, and you are able to sense when to step back and expand the original idea to fuel the process more. Expand and contract. Breathe in, breathe out.

Think of an elite athlete like Golden State Warriors' superstar Stephen Curry. There are nights when he seems to be playing the game at a higher level than everyone else on the court. He passes without eyes. He shoots without thought. He dribbles with ten hands. We say he's in the zone. We call him an artist, a genius, a magician. We exclaim that he created "an unforgettable, unbelievable, undeniable masterpiece moment. . . . Curry transcended the game." LeBron James tweets: "@StephenCurry30 needs to stop it man!! He's ridiculous man! Never before seen someone like him in the history of ball!"

Curry's rise to the supernatural is all the more profound when you understand how he actually does it. He was not expected to amount to much at a mere six foot three and 185 pounds. The 2009 NBA Scouting Report on him read as follows:

> Weaknesses: Far below NBA standard in regard to explosiveness and athleticism . . . extremely small for the NBA shooting guard position, and it will likely keep him from being much of a defender at the next level . . . not a natural point guard that an NBA team can rely on to run a team . . . Can overshoot and rush into shots from time to time . . . Will have to adjust to not being a volume shooter which could have an effect on his effectiveness . . . Doesn't like when defenses are too physical with him . . . Not a great finisher around the basket due to his size and physical attributes . . . Makes some silly mistakes at the PG position.

Truth is, had Curry not learned to trust the creative process and evolve into who he is today, that scouting report would have likely proved accurate. But Curry has become what New York's Drake

Baer calls "an extreme outlier . . . in his ability to process sensory input. . . . In simplistic terms, he's seeing more of the game, allowing him to exploit opponents' positioning to create shots, find passing lanes, and force turnovers. . . . Curry is something of [a] poster boy for an [sic] new era in sports, where superior neural circuitry is regarded as just as much of an advantage as a higher vertical or a sweeter jump shot."

Steph Curry didn't get this way overnight. He's a Grinder who saw the need to become a different sort of player, a more cerebral one who can see more opportunities and seize more advantages than his opponents. Then he worked his butt off to get there. According to Curry, that hard work has allowed him to "feel more creative on the floor . . . so I can make better moves and have more control over my space out there." In other words, says Baer, Curry has trained his brain and body to create opportunities out of thin air.

The sum of trusting a fluid creative process is that you set out to shape and become rather than to solidify or confirm. This small difference is so impactful because it immediately changes your expectations.

Grinders transition away from expectations that are governed by the success and failure of individual products or pursuits. Instead they are free to allow their work to gain more and more momentum, which evolves into something clearer, better, and more affecting than the original results they sought.

Igniters transition away from unrealistic expectations that never materialize beyond the surfaces of whiteboards and Moleskines. Instead, they are free to constantly work out their big ideas, not only into tangible products, but also into products that ignite bigger and better ideas.

Both Grinders and Igniters transition into expectations that are governed by constant effort, education, and growth. You become, to use Dostoevsky's phrase, "engaged in full-time engineering." As a result, you are constantly learning, evolving, and creating. The product in focus—if there currently is one—is not your end product and it does not define you. It is merely a measure of your progress, either through success or failure, along the frontier of constant iteration.

This is something Mr. Bushnell seemed to learn after the Cheese.

In an article for *Fast Company*, journalist Benj Edwards recounts the next chapter in Bushnell's entrepreneurial journey, which began when one of his friends, Stan Honey, invited him to sail in the 1983 Transpacific Yacht Race from Los Angeles to Honolulu. Honey was a gifted engineer whose day job was working for the Silicon Valley research institute SRI International. Knowing his friend's skills, Bushnell commissioned Honey to create one of the first computer-based navigation systems to use on their yacht during the race.

Early one morning during the race, explains Edwards, the two friends were on night watch together and they implemented Honey's system to "get a fix on their location." Keep in mind, this was pre-GPS. At the time, the common way to track a ship's location was to rely on a visual of a satellite orbiting the Earth, which occurred every twelve hours. The obvious problem was that the satellite orientation could not pin their location frequently enough to keep them from going way off course between twelve-hour check-ins. To track their yacht's whereabouts more regularly, Honey's system calculated their position "based on the ancient techniques of celestial navigation, using a sextant, and of dead reckoning, which involves keeping track of distance and direction traveled and as compared to a previously known location." Honey was essentially calibrating their whereabouts using the ever-changing position of the stars.

These mapping methods, while archaic by today's standards, were so impressive that not only did Honey and Bushnell's yacht eventually win the Transpacific Yacht Race, they ignited a major spark of an idea during those predawn hours.

Bushnell and Honey got to chatting about other ways to use the navigational system on land. Honey suggested a navigation system for cars. Bushnell immediately saw the genius in the idea, and shortly thereafter he gave Honey $500,000 in seed money to create a prototype. A digital mapping company was born.

The company's "Navigator" system was the first commercially available and viable automotive navigation system. As aid from satellites was not yet available, the system relied on a rear windshield compass and strategically placed sensors on two of the cars wheels to track speed, distance, and direction. The team of engineers, headed by Honey, then created a driver-centric display that moved around a central fixed point on the screen that represented the car. When the Navigator was finally ready to go to market, says Edwards, it worked so well that users thought they were being tricked. They didn't believe such a device could actually exist in the 1980s.

Product sales grew slowly at first but steadily enough that the company changed hands several times over the years, growing in price each time as the value of its mapping data and navigational patents became more and more apparent. The product's capabilities evolved as well. The initial spark fueled a grind that remained open to sparks. This was different from Bushnell's previous ventures, where the grind blinded him to two massive sparks. This difference was paramount to both the growth and the lasting success of Honey and Bushnell's navigation system, which predated the modern GPS capabilities we know today by fifteen years. "It was so early," writes Edwards, "that its inventors had to digitize their own maps and figure out how to get them into an automobile in an era before solid-state mass storage, optical discs, or wireless Internet was available to do the job. (The solution: special tape cassettes.)"

As GPS became available in 1995—initially with restrictions to protect against America's enemies misusing it—Honey and Bushnell's navigation system was updated and improved. When Sony acquired their industry-leading company a year later, the price was approximately $100 million. The company eventually became a part of TomTom for a price tag of $2.9 billion, which ensured that its map data, some of it originally digitized in 1984, would live on to this day.

Bushnell stuck with the creative process in Navigator's journey. While it may not be the legacy he's known for today—pop culture has a lot to do with that—the car navigation system was the longest lasting of Bushnell's sparks. Perhaps it's no coincidence that the company, which was originally headquartered in Sunnyvale, California, eventually moved to another California city that shares a name with a famous New Jersey locale that was known to be a bastion of innovation and creativity: Menlo Park. Perhaps it's also no coincidence that the company's name, Etak, was derived from a Polynesian word that means "navigating intuitively by the stars."

Early in his career, Bushnell was a young Grinder who missed some big sparks that flew along the way. But it seems that by the time the Navigator came around, he'd learned to embrace the Igniter in him, too. Instead of solely focusing on the finish line or the manifestation of the original product, he and Stan Honey remained open to the expansion of the initial spark.

I learned a similar lesson after losing my business. I, too, was a young Grinder who missed the flying sparks along the way. Looking back, I can see now where I could have evolved my business to perhaps weather the dot-com storm and eventually realize the bounty that the top speakers' bureaus are now reaping from today's multibillion-dollar pot. But all I knew back then was hard work— and hard work wasn't enough. Still, I don't look back with regrets. I wouldn't be where I am today without my oversight. Bushnell might say the same thing. Sure, I'd like to have figured out a way to keep that flame alive, but the truth is that the ashes of that blaze are what cleared the way for a bigger idea and greater growth.

Prescribed burns are controlled fires that remove dead material and increase the exposure of bare soil, the good stuff that allows widespread growth. In 2010, two researchers studied prescribed burns on Colorado's Pawnee National Grassland and found that "except after severe drought, prescribed burns done during late winter . . . increase forage protein content, starting with the first spring after burning." In a related earlier study, the same researchers found that prescribed burning actually enhanced the digestibility of certain grasses.

Controlled burning stimulates the germination of desirable forest trees, thus renewing the forest. In fact, some seeds, like that of the sequoia tree, remain dormant until fire breaks down the seed coating. Prescribed burns not only renew the Earth's soil so that new seeds can spring up; they also prevent catastrophic wildfires that destroy everything in their path.

In Florida, during the drought in 1998, wildfires incinerated hundreds of homes over the course of nearly two months. More than 45,000 people were evacuated and fire suppression organizations from 44 states responded. To reduce the damage as much as possible, Florida hosted the largest aerial suppression operation ever conducted in the United States. Largely because of this massive effort, protection of structures was quite successful, with only 337 homes damaged or destroyed and 33 businesses burned. However, the damage could have been far less; it could have even been eliminated entirely.

When the ash had finally settled, forestry managers in the area noted that the underlying cause was prior cessation of annual controlled burning. Many homeowners in the area had complained about the smoke smell in the air some five to ten days per year. Out of courtesy, the controlled burns were stopped, leaving the area highly susceptible to damage and loss.

Don't make the same mistake and shy away from greater ignition. Not only will you—like me—leave yourself susceptible to an enormous meltdown, you will stall and even stop the growth of better ideas inside and around you.

Whether you have no idea or a big idea you're already grinding out, press forward. You have to regularly ignite fires to constantly unearth the best seeds. And you must also not forget to step back from the fire you're fueling and look around. Within the scattered sparks and embers, new signs of growth and better paths for progress emerge.

Trust this.

2

ATTACH YOURSELF
TO THE WORK

It is not what the artist does that counts. But what he is.

—**Pablo Picasso**

ROBERT FROST ONCE SAID THAT INDIVIDUAL CREATION begins with knowing your own bone. "Pursue, keep up with, circle round and round your life," he said. "Know your own bone: gnaw at it, bury it, unearth it, and gnaw at it still."

Do you know your own bone?

What is it that distinguishes you from everyone else, and your existence from everyone else's you know?

That's your creative wellspring. Be willing not only to answer the questions but also to live from the answers, especially when little about life seems clear or particularly fulfilling.

In the age we live in, you aren't trained to draw from this deep well. It seems too mysterious, too messy, too mushy . . . too time consuming. Instead, you are led to believe that the path to creative distinction begins with first studying who and what works and then setting out to emulate them or that—not first examining yourself or what's inside you. "The idea of research has often made painting go astray," asserted Picasso in 1923, "and made the artist lose himself in mental lucubrations."

The true act of creation doesn't ask that you not learn from others or other things, or be inspired by them or, to use Picasso's word, research them. You can and should allow external influences to be educators in your efforts to become a better creator. Your environment is a constant source of learning, a constant source of "mental lucubrations." But you can't get caught up there. It's a slippery slope that deposits you into the shallow end of your existence.

External influences cannot be your only source of creative inspiration, let alone your primary one. If they are, your creations will struggle to be both distinctive and personally affecting. What you need, and what the world needs, is you incarnated into creative forms.

Creation is origination, which stems from originality. Creation can be inspired by the originality of others, including the natural world. But constant creation requires you to travel beyond restylized mimicry. The brilliant writer Julia Cameron says our original voices are often muffled and even strangled by other people's expectations. To be a constant creator you can never let what makes you original and distinct be snuffed out.

Why?

"We do not see our size," writes Cameron. "We do not view ourselves with accuracy. We are far larger, far more marvelous, far more deeply and consistently creative than we recognize or know. We do not credit ourselves with what it is we can—and often do—accomplish."

To ignite sparks—your truest and most authentic ones—you must first find your own bone, not everyone else's, not pop culture's, not the market's. If research must be done into what you can and should create, let it begin in the name of finding your own bone. When you find that, you tap your strongest and most constant source of fuel that drives you to grind hard whenever and wherever you need to.

To grind your sparks and spark your grind . . .
ATTACH YOURSELF TO THE WORK

The single greatest benefit in being a constant creator is that the process doesn't just improve what you create, it improves who you are. There is a transcendent need in every one of us to become all we were created to be. At the heart of this is what we do with what we have.

Although we don't know all the details up front, we have a drive to step into the mystery of our own potential. Who can I become? What can I accomplish? What impact can I have? We never lose this drive. We can suppress it, but deep down we always wonder. "In one way or another," writes Frederick Buechner, "man comes upon mystery as a summons to pilgrimage . . . where he glimpses a destination that he can never know fully until he reaches it."

When you embrace the creative process each day, you are embracing the becoming of your potential. You can admit that you don't know what all this means while still welcoming the prospect—not only of seeing what you can do but of what you will become along the way. Oxford professor and creator of *The Chronicles of Narnia*, C. S. Lewis called this unceasing wonder your "true north." It points to your destiny—what you are meant to be and do—and you are drawn to both its mystery and its fulfillment. How you handle that attraction is up to you, however.

In *On Writing Well*, author William Zinsser explains the temptation creators (in his experience, writers) face when they sit down to create. "They are driven by a compulsion to put some sort of themselves on paper, and yet they don't just write what comes naturally. They sit down to commit an act of literature, and the self who emerges on paper is far stiffer than the person who sat down to write. . . . [Yet] ultimately the product that any writer has to sell is not the subject written about, but who he or she is."

With any of your ideas and the subsequent works in which they are embodied, there is a temptation to edit them into a form that is more acceptable to others. The temptation has won when you've completely edited yourself out of your creations. Consider how much easier this has become in the digital age we live in today. The many forms of social media allow us—as individuals and companies—to brand ourselves in inauthentic ways. There are no laws keeping us from hiding our flaws and painting ourselves in a prettier light than we really are.

Ads make products look like invitations to a dream life. Tweets make people look better and sound smarter, cleverer and more hip. How is it that everyone on LinkedIn is the Chief Something: Chief Love Giver or Chief Idea Ninja or Chief Thought Leader? Why can't we just be what we really are—managers or sales executives or customer service reps? While we all possess these beautifully unique personal brands that have intrinsic value, we often maintain an unhealthy desire to be acceptable to others more than we wish to be true to ourselves. That creates a constant temptation to conform to others' understanding of what's valuable. If we give in to it, we make creations that are detached from our original selves and our authentic voices.

We think this is the easier, the simpler, and the least messy way to just get shit done—whether that's impressing friends, launching businesses, or selling more products. As a result, we end up ignoring those deeper fires. We quiet those embers until they are fully extinguished.

In a 2011 article for *Harvard Business Review,* corporate coach Gill Corkindale argues the case for detachment from your work. In her piece, Corkindale describes once sitting next to a woman on a plane to New York who unloaded her entire work history over the course of the flight. Corkindale was exhausted by the experience, which she admits came about because she asked one harmless question: "What do you do?" Head throbbing as she exited the plane, Corkindale took note to be more careful about asking the question again—especially while stuck next to the responder for multiple hours.

Several years later, during a flight to Zurich, Corkindale became that very same woman when her seatmate asked her the same question. The lesson she derived from the two experiences is that we ought to learn to detach ourselves and our identities from our work. "It is very easy," she writes, "to be consumed by work and consequently become crashing bores."

Her advice to readers followed suit. "Treat time outside work as sacrosanct and refresh yourself. . . . Remind yourself that you are much more than your job."

While her advice is considerate, well meaning, and well received by many, it is not the way of constant creativity. Corkindale and many corporate coaches like her make a good case if you're struggling with the idea of work-life balance. However, the assumption underlying every piece of work-life balance advice—and thus every piece of advice about being detached from work—is that we don't want our work to consume us. Work is just that, work. It's necessary, and if we're lucky, diligent, or both, work provides us a nice lifestyle and enough physical and emotional margin to enjoy life off the job. We then lead two separate lives that we do our best to balance with each other so that neither undermines the value of the other.

This sounds awful, if you ask me. Especially what this attitude means for work.

Is that the best we can do?

The majority of work-life balance advice concedes the hours on the job, as if to say, *We can do nothing better with them.* And this is the problem with the argument for being detached from your work responsibilities, or anything you do on the clock, for that matter.

Why can't what we do, what we create, consume us? Why shouldn't we want to be caught up in all that we do with our lives? Isn't that the essence of living with passion and purpose? Isn't this why Federico Fellini asserted it was only when he was working that he felt truly alive, that he felt like he was having sex? Or why greats like baseball Hall of Famer Ernie Banks and writer Ray Bradbury and inventor Thomas Edison all offered the same response when asked about their work: "Work? I never worked a day in my life. I always loved what I was doing, had a passion for it," "I never worked a day in my life. I just played," "I never did a day's work in my life. It was all fun."

"The ideal of compartmentalizing our work and home lives sounds appealing in a self-help book or advice-based TV show," writes psychologist Christian Jarrett, "but reality is much messier than that. As anyone who has ever received a call from their child's school at work knows, the barrier between our professional and domestic realms is more of a door than a wall. Emotional traffic through that door moves in both directions."

Dr. Jarrett cites the findings of three European psychologists, Ana Isabel Sanz-Vergel, Alfredo Rodríguez-Muñoz, and Karina Nielsen, who studied the diaries kept by approximately 150 employees at 25 Spanish organizations. In their paper, which appears in the March 2015 issue of the *Journal of Occupational and Organizational Psychology,* the researchers documented a common occurrence, "what they described as a 'negative spiral' [that] started with a clash of priorities between work and home . . . followed by an increased risk of arguments with colleagues at work [which] then fed back and increased domestic friction in the home."

Jarrett's conclusion?

"Although you have many different roles in life, you are ultimately one and the same person, with limited time, energy and resources."

What if instead of conceding half of your waking hours—which, to Dr. Jarrett's point, is pretty pointless because life inevitably runs together anyway—you dove headlong into all the hours of your day and made them all life giving?

This is the essence of attachment. And it's the only approach that will turn the roles you play into spark-inducing ventures.

When you attach yourself to everything you do, you manifest pieces of your being into your everyday living. Some of these creations are practice, warm-ups for a bigger manifestation. They won't all feel warm and fuzzy and ultrafulfilling. But all creations are lessons that create momentum if we're willing to capture it. A few of them will ignite into flames that spread and come to mean more to you than the feeling that you are well balanced.

"Knowledge is only a rumor," goes a saying from the Asaro tribe of Indonesia, "until it lives in the muscle." You can talk about passion and purpose all day long. You might even feel you have a solid sense of them in your own life. But passion and purpose are just an unproven notion until they are lived out in the creative muscles you use every day. When this happens, your life begins to make sense because what is inside you is integrated into what comes from you to the outside world. You also become a more potent force in what you do. A recent and great example of this effect is seen in the story of Dr. Bennet Omalu, the subject of the book turned feature film *Concussion.*

In Jeanne Marie Laskas's game-changing book, she illuminates the epic sort of Grinder Dr. Omalu was during his rise to the pivotal position of forensic pathologist-in-training at the Allegheny County coroner's office in Pittsburgh and beyond (he is currently chief medical examiner of San Joaquin County, California). He holds seven degrees, including an MBA, and is board certified to practice for different disciplines of pathology: anatomic, clinical, forensic, and neuropathology.

But what most who knew Dr. Omalu didn't know, until he encountered the body of deceased Pittsburgh Steelers legend Mike Webster in 2002, was that he was also deeply attached to his work. At the time of his life's intersection with the death of Mike Webster, Bennet Omalu was considered, despite all his training to that point, a rookie in the field of forensic neuropathology. Yet his profound, authentic attachment to his grind ignited one of the biggest and most important infernos in the history of sports.

Dr. Omalu had never given the NFL a minute of attention before meeting Mike Webster. Never seen a game. Didn't even know what a Steeler was, let alone who this famous player was that everyone was talking about. Still, writes Laskas, "Bennet grew to love Mike Webster."

After that fateful meeting in the Allegheny County morgue, reports of Webster's exploits on the field and his tragic derailment after retiring were impossible to ignore—especially in the city that worshipped him as a player for a decade and a half. However, the primary messages Omalu heard were disheartening to him. He heard that Mike Webster was a Hall of Famer, a nine-time Pro Bowler, and a four-time Super Bowl champ. He also heard that he was known as "Iron Mike," and that he blew his money and fame, made terrible decisions, and eventually threw his life away on drugs. People made fun of him, demeaned him, derogated him. What a shame, they said, to waste such a career. To waste the opportunities it provided. To waste the love and admiration of an entire city, an entire sport. These merciless comments didn't sit well with the doctor who had been charged to find Webster's cause of death.

"They wheeled the body in," writes Laskas, ". . . just a gray corpse wearing jeans. No shirt. No shoes. . . . Bennet put on his rubber apron and his plastic face shield and his headset and turned the music up: Teddy Pendergrass, Bob Marley, Julio Iglesias. He lined up his instruments. He was easily the most meticulous medical examiner in the morgue; this was, after all, his art. He was the Michael Jackson of autopsy."

Once he was prepped, Omalu propped up Webster's head and spoke to him out loud, with understanding and compassion. "Mike, you have been misjudged," the doctor said. "It is not right. . . . Let me use my education to establish the truth. Let us vindicate you."

As Laskas points out, there was no outside sense of urgency to determine what killed Mike Webster. He'd been found dead of a heart attack in the rundown car he'd been living in, surrounded by bottles of pills, wearing physical signs of drug abuse and thick scars on his thigh from self-inflicted Taser strikes to combat insomnia.

Although his death wasn't a suicide, most believed he'd essentially performed his own sad, drawn-out assisted suicide. Webster had lost his mind in the years before his death, displaying regular signs of schizophrenia and bipolar disorder. Most assumed this was the result of a depression and drugs spiral.

But this was the detached answer, the checklist conclusion. Omalu didn't assume. He had more than his head in Webster's autopsy. His whole being was in it. The truth about Mike Webster's death would only come about from its collision with Dr. Omalu's life, his passion and purpose, his attachment to his work. "Omalu had always fancied himself an advocate for the dead," writes Laskas in the 2009 *GQ* article that spawned the book. "That's how he viewed his job. . . . A forensic pathologist was charged with defending and speaking for the departed."

Laskas notes that after several days of looking at small slices of Webster's brain under a microscope in the morgue, Omalu placed the former hero's brain in a plastic tub and took it home, where he set up shop on a table in the corner of his living room. There he not only continued cutting slides to study, he further educated himself "on trauma, on football, on helmets, on Alzheimer's disease, on concussions, on impact, on g-force, on protein accumulation, on dementia pugilistica. . . . It became for him a calling. He was after all a spiritual man, and he came to know Mike Webster in the most personal way. 'Help me' is what he heard Mike Webster say."

Omalu had no idea what this calling would require of him. But he was no less committed to forging the path. His attachment to his work gave him the psychological, physical, and spiritual resolve to overcome any adversity along the way, which in Omalu's case spanned the full spectrum from detractors to death threats. And when a person is committed to a craft come hell or high water, sparks will continue to fly. Eventually they will start a blaze.

In the late nineteenth century, German philosopher Friedrich Nietzsche penned the phrase: "When one has one's *wherefore* of life, one gets along with almost every *how.*" It wasn't popularized, however, until an Austrian psychologist cited the line in a book he published in 1946, the year after he survived the Holocaust. The book was originally called *Say "Yes" to Life: A Psychologist Experiences the Concentration Camp* but was later changed to *Man's Search for Meaning,* and is one of the best-selling books of all time. In its pages, the author Viktor Frankl credits his Holocaust survival with an ability to grasp a purpose while there, which for him meant helping others in the concentration camp survive, and dignifying the deaths of those who would not.

Clearly, having a purpose is good for our psychological health. But how it works is significant to the life of a constant creator. Popular British psychologist, lecturer, and author Steve Taylor explains that having a purpose that attaches us to what we do each day "makes us less vulnerable to . . . 'psychological discord.' . . . the fundamental sense of unease . . . which can manifest itself in boredom, anxiety and depression." In other words, "purpose means that we spend less time immersed in the associational chatter of our minds." Purpose, he continues, also makes us less self-centered. When we feel that our actions are a part of something larger going on, part of a bigger production, this deters us from latching onto our worries and fears.

Ultimately, when we feel a sense of purpose in something we are doing, we're "manifesting the creative urge of evolution, becoming its expression." We are participating in the growing progress and improvement not only of our existence but of the whole environment in which our lives play out.

This is a common theme in most major spiritual disciplines. When we attach a purpose to what we do, we are able to attain a state in which we are driven by what is best and right, not necessarily by a particular deadline or outcome, but more accurately by the best path. We are motivated to steward our skills, surrender our artistic gifts, to God's plan, to the greatest good of those around us, to the highest end, which is when we take our last breath. We cannot be satisfied simply because the project is completed or the product is on the shelves.

Of course, along the way we reach destinations, and some are milestones. We are rewarded with joy and fulfillment in them. But if we are constant creators, attached to our work, what we do is a continual construction, a growing manifestation, and there is joy and fulfillment in this alone because it is wholly linked to being and becoming what and who we are. As you and I create, we and the world in which we live are also being created. By creating from a place of authenticity—offering what you alone can offer, and continuing to do so—you take place in the re-creation of your world. Or perhaps the word is more appropriately written as "recreation." This is no coincidence.

When who you are comes through in what you produce, the production no longer feels like work. Even when the hours are long.

This is what drove—and drives to this day—Dr. Bennet Omalu.

Had he not attached himself to his work, it is unlikely he would have seen his highly disruptive brainchild through. It's also unlikely the entire sports world would now be working toward protecting millions of athletes from head injuries that can destroy their lives.

It took several weeks for Dr. Omalu to grind out the spark that got the fire burning in this field, but when he did, his resolve would not allow it to be snuffed out. When Omalu finally discovered in Mike Webster's fifty-year-old brain the signs that best compared to advanced Alzheimer's in a ninety-year-old patient, he immediately showed the slides to his well-known supervisor Cyril Wecht and to a handful of neuroscientists at the University of Pittsburgh. They concurred that what they were looking at was a new disease that no one had seen or documented before. Dr. Omalu had to name it, they said. He called it chronic traumatic encephalopathy (CTE) and then wrote an article on his findings titled "Chronic Traumatic Encephalopathy in a National Football League Player." Omalu sent it to the most respected neurology journal to be published. He expected excitement from the NFL doctors for whom he felt he had done a great service in discovering this terrible disease, which they could now work to prevent.

Dr. Omalu was sadly mistaken. NFL doctors deemed his report false and called for its retraction. It was not retracted. But it wouldn't have mattered either way. This was now part of Omalu as much as it was of Mike Webster. In fact, this was all his to see through. He continued grinding, undaunted by the adversity, ignited by passion and purpose.

A detached doctor would not have seen it through. There was too much at stake. A great job. A growing family. A dream home. A respected mentor.

If you've seen the film, you know that Dr. Omalu was pressured to back down from his discovery. He didn't. In fact, he sparked more proof from the premature deaths of three more NFL players. As a result, the collateral damage increased as the enemies of his revelations fought fire with fire. Eventually, after Omalu's wife suffered a miscarriage upon finding she was being stalked, and after Omalu's mentor Dr. Wecht was forced to resign, the doctor made the difficult decision to sell his family's dream home outside Pittsburgh and move to northern California for a job with the San Joaquin County coroner's office. All the while, the blaze he started burned.

When former NFL Players Association executive Dave Duerson took his own life in February 2011 due to growing cognitive issues, admitting in his suicide note that Omalu was right, Omalu's adversaries came under heated scrutiny to reckon with his discoveries. Three months later, neurologists at Boston University confirmed that Duerson suffered from CTE.

That small spark that arose from Omalu's deep-seated work still burns bright today. The NFL is now working alongside doctors, researchers, and engineers to construct the right resolutions for early diagnosis, proper treatment, and ultimately the mitigation of traumatic head injuries in the game of football and beyond.

Meanwhile, Omalu continues his hands-on work with autopsies, speaking as an advocate for the deceased—grinding out his calling. It is perhaps fitting that his surname, Omalu, is shortened from Onyemalukwube, which translates: If you know, come forth and speak. His story is an inspiring demonstration to all of us that it is completely possible to have a nontraditionally creative job and still do highly creative, highly influential work.

———

Your greatest creative impetus is the attachment of who you are to what you do. This is, to use Picasso's words, what counts. Detachment doesn't automatically spell failure. It just makes the grind much more grindlike; you become driven by destinations rather than destiny. And what if the destinations don't satisfy you in your deepest parts? Or worse, what if you travel so far from who you are that you forget what makes you come alive? Fyodor Dostoevsky alluded to this ominous outcome in *The House of the Dead* when he wrote, "If one wanted to crush, to annihilate a man utterly, to inflict on him the most terrible of punishments so that the most ferocious murderer would shudder at it and dread it beforehand, one need only give him work of an absolutely, completely useless and irrational character."

Detachment forces you to be driven by singular goals rather than by growth. To be roused by an ever-fleeting endgame. In this state, your work is more difficult to weave together into one inspiring tapestry.

On the other hand, when who you are is attached to what you do, striving for excellence excites you instead of burdening you. Your drive to see an endeavor through is fueled by passion and purpose instead of mere duty or obligation. There's a tangible difference. Often it's subtle at the outset. But over time, it bears out. Detachment is the short path to frustration, burnout, and boredom. Attachment is the short path to discovery, growth, and fulfillment.

Of the two, attachment is the only path to mastery. And mastery, writes Museum of Modern Art curator Sarah Lewis in *The Rise: Creativity, the Gift of Failure, and the Search for Mastery,* "requires endurance. . . . [It] is not the equivalent of what we might consider its cognate—*perfectionism*—an inhuman aim motivated by a concern with how others view us. Mastery is also not the same as success— an event-based victory based on a peak point, a punctuated moment in time. Mastery is not merely a commitment to a goal, but to a curved-line, constant pursuit."

You are not a static figure at a fixed point in time. Although we all like to be known by and for something, with the exception of your genetic traits, who you are and what you do are constantly evolving. When you lean into this dynamic reality rather than trying to grasp at a static identity, you attach yourself to what can still be, to what is still becoming—which is greatly influenced by your daily creations. And nothing allows you to explore and affirm your identity like your creations.

Winston Churchill once said that at first we shape our life's work and then it shapes us. He meant that positively, as an indication of how our aspirations, once done, eventually reshape us in positive ways we didn't imagine at the outset. This is true only if we are attached to what we do. If we are not, Churchill's words take on a different, but equally true, meaning, as if he were saying that we set about our work with good intentions but that work overtakes us and reshapes us into something we are not.

Which is more true of you today?

Your answer is an indication of your level of attachment and thus your ability to ignite authentic sparks from your grind.

Is your grind shaping you positively or negatively? Ask yourself the question: Do my sparks inspire me, personally . . . or are they someone else's sparks?

Your creations are meant to shape you in good ways, into better, more advanced versions of yourself. "Work is at the center of our lives and influences who we are and all that we do," writes Al Gini. "Work is not just about earning a livelihood. It is not just about getting paid, about gainful employment. Nor is it only about the use of one's mind and body to accomplish a specific task or project. Work is also one of the most significant contributing factors to one's inner life and development. . . . [I]t literally names us, identifies us, to both ourselves and others."

We tend to downplay our own originality, especially when it comes to offering it to the world in tangible form. But if we all thought the same thoughts and carried out the same acts in a similar manner, there would be no innovation, progress would be predictable at best, and we'd eventually be bored out of our minds. (It might be the reason you're bored now.)

The idea of a well-oiled machine is actually a precarious scenario—in a company and especially in an individual. While it's great to be efficient, we can never make efficiency a priority over effectiveness. And constant effectiveness requires an ever-flowing stream of creativity.

Detachment looks and feels effective. At first. But soon it's the epitome of ineffectiveness—disconnected parts moving in different directions at a different pace with different objectives. It's the proverbial right hand unaware of what the left hand is doing. Except in reality it's your head and heart that are estranged.

I don't believe most do this intentionally. It usually just happens. Life becomes demanding, and we respond in what seems like the most efficient manner, according to the needs and opportunities of the moment, with the most accessible resources we possess. We react practically but not intuitively. We fail to consider our deepest need for cohesiveness, for our inner lives to be aligned with our outer lives. As a result, we rarely notice that our greatest opportunity—in any opportunity—is to embody the words and actions that only we can.

"We . . . want to be the poets of our lives," wrote Nietzsche, "and first of all in the smallest and most commonplace matters," then in ways that craft our legacies and greater opportunities for those in our wake. The question is whether you are willing to ignite the moments of your life from your heart and soul, not just your head and hands.

"Here is my secret. It's quite simple," wrote iconic French writer and aviator Antoine de Saint-Exupéry. "One sees clearly only with the heart. Anything essential is invisible to the eyes."

The essence of sparking your grind, which will allow you to grind longer and harder, is allowing the deep and boiling pools within you to boil over in your words and actions and thus frame and construct your creations. This doesn't mean that you should silence your head. Intellect and insight are needed, too. Your brain is wired for efficiency. It's a survival mechanism that you need at work. But you must allow your deeper self to speak and see and guide. When you do, it not only changes the effect of your works, but it also amps up the very nature of your motivation. Your inner, heart-led drive is stronger and burns hotter than any reasoning. To paraphrase Saint-Exupéry in *Citadelle*, if you want to build a ship, don't summon people to tasks and work, but instead teach them to long for the vastness of the sea. Longing, desire, purpose—these are the hottest creative embers inside us, and when we free them up, they forge our best creations, daily and over time.

This is a lesson I had to learn the hard way, through a harsh loss that illuminated the deficiency in my headfirst approach to the works of my hands. The void left me wondering that C. S. Lewis kind of wondering, about true north. From that vantage point, a career I'd have told you a year earlier was my sweet spot was stripped naked of all logical adornments. What was left was little that moved me purely and deeply.

Sure, I'd been happy. I'd have probably told you I was utterly fulfilled at the height of my success. Tasha and I could largely do what we wanted. We had nice things. Took nice trips. Had a nice environment in which to raise our boys. But the truth was that I was just basking in the benefits of hard work. Nothing wrong with that initially—but because the pursuit was detached from who I was inside, a big disappointment, really a reckoning, was bound to happen.

There was an artist in me waiting, no, begging to emerge. He'd been belittled when I was young, debased through traditional education, then bullied out of sight through eight years of harvesting my hard-line grind. But after losing the harvest in what felt like one fell swoop, I wanted to be honest. I needed to be.

I huddled with Tasha and decided I needed to unplug. Just go cold turkey and stop worrying about stocks or fretting over the shrinking bank account. I gave Tasha all the financial responsibilities that had fed and defined me before.

For the first time in my life I was free to seek new inspiration—so I enrolled in art classes. I can't emphasize enough how unusual this was for me. Remember, I was a suit-and-tie guy, a salesman and an agent. The last time I'd drawn or painted was in grade school. My teacher bluntly told me I lacked talent. Her criticism, which was intended to guide me, had a debilitating effect. I avoided anything remotely resembling art or creativity.

We all have points in our life when a new or renewed activity can lead us to breakthroughs and spark genuine innovation, but here's what I've learned. When you're first dipping your toe in a new body of water, it won't seem anything like a breakthrough. Indeed, it will often look and feel like an ordinary hobby, even a silly urge. Well-meaning friends and relatives might shake their heads at your enthusiasm, might suggest that you've lost your focus or that you're wasting your time. Most people are conditioned to judge value only according to the end product or the material results, but you have to shift the paradigm. This is your journey, not theirs—God bless the pragmatists in our lives. This is the very point at which you have to trust the eyes of your heart—even when you're the only one who sees the spark.

Art suddenly spoke to me because it was the antithesis of my previous life, but the truth is that I realized I'd been devaluing art and creativity my entire adult life. Money was not the primary metric in my artistic pursuit, and I noticed that everyone seemed to define art differently. The openness and infinite scale of possibilities spoke to me. So I didn't just dip in a toe, I cannonballed in.

I spent my days, six to eight hours every day, with other artists, painting. We'd have a model and an instructor, and we'd just paint and paint some more and then talk about painting. I found myself enjoying artists, the way they think, the way they view life, imagination, and social issues. I respected them even though no one was taking this art class to build a business and conquer an industry—really, because of that. My classmates were painting because they wanted to feel something different and become something more. I was there for similar reasons but I initially fought against my need for measured progress. I'd get down on myself and compare my work to others that I considered much better.

I especially struggled to draw hands. "That's your ego speaking," my teachers would say. "If you can block your ego and paint what you see, you'll unlock your art." I listened and I learned that my eyes often deceived me. I learned that there's a difference between the way we think we see ourselves and the way we actually are. Our eyesight will actually create optical illusions and cognitive biases that don't exist in ourselves or in nature.

Take the face. It isn't round. It's oval. There are no straight lines in nature. The human body is more of an S; it stands in this beautiful, curving shape. Then, of course, shapes change as they capture light. I accepted that my eyes could trick me. I started closing them and then I could see infinity. I could see truth. This is how I learned to paint.

When describing the inception of a writing project, Steven Pressfield says, "Something seizes me. I become hooked. . . . You don't know why. . . . But you're smitten and you know it." Then, says Pressfield, the creator has to go beyond this. "He has to ask himself (and not let go till he has the answer): 'What *exactly* am I in love with? What's *the essence* of it?'"

You must ask the same question, and not let go of your answer, if you want to spark your grind every day—if you want your work to be more than rote labor that is detached from life. Let the fires within you point the way and inspire your words and deeds. Close your eyelids if you have to. And your eyes will be opened.

———

Attaching yourself to your work is not capturing a glowing mission and vision statement. While it's not a bad place to begin, the real attachment happens when you begin living out those ideas, when you begin actively loving the thing you've fallen in love with. As you know, loving anything isn't all hugs and kisses—but thank God it begins there.

We are known largely by what we do. Our creations define us, name us: a great compliment for those whose work springs from within them; a great disappointment to those whose work is detached from who they are. So many of us just do. The more detached our doing is from our being, the more rote our activity becomes, the less we are known by others. Passion is missing. There is no deep meaning. No driving desire to be creative beyond meeting expectations.

Detachment is a necessity, the only necessity, when all you seek is the endgame in the quickest manner possible. It's not enough, however, when you seek transcendence from your works—a creation that reaches far and wide, and a game that doesn't end until you take your last breath.

There's a scene in the film *The Legend of Bagger Vance,* based on Pressfield's novel, that provides a memorable depiction of the struggle to create from our truest selves and the ultimate freedom we realize when we finally do. The main character, Rannulph Junuh, is a former golf prodigy who went off to World War I and lost himself—everything he knew and believed about himself, including his once brilliant ability to swing the club. But not long after returning from the war to his hometown of Savannah, Georgia, he is asked to play in a unique but very important golf tournament involving only three players: himself and the two greatest players in the world, Walter Hagen and Bobby Jones.

Junuh laughs off the request but the people of the city persist and, reluctantly, he caves.

Then, with the help of a mysterious caddie named Bagger Vance, who appears out of nowhere, Junuh prepares for the tournament as best he can. But the preparation is not enough. After one round Junuh is already way behind. And it only gets worse. He's painful to watch. Hooks, shanks, duffs, missed putts, one after the other, with an occasional good shot that only gets his hopes up. But Bagger knows something Junuh is not yet ready to consider. Before it's too late, he steps in and helps the lost soul accurately see his life and the opportunities before him.

> There's a perfect shot trying to find every one of us. All we got to do is get ourselves out of its way . . . and let it choose us. . . . You can't see that flag as some dragon you got to slay. You've got to look with soft eyes. See the place where the tides, and the seasons . . . the turning of the earth . . . all come together. Where everything that is . . . becomes one. You've got to seek that place with your soul, Junuh. . . . It's just you . . . that ball . . . that flag . . . and all you are. . . . The home of your authentic swing.

If you've seen the film, you know that from the next swing forward, Junuh begins to return to authentic form, not just as a golfer but as a man who discovers purpose in life again. When the three reach the final hole, Junuh has pulled even with the pros and he's playing his best golf. He lashes a long drive off the tee that sets him up with as good a chance as any to miraculously win the hole and the match. But as he stands over his ball preparing to take his approach shot, Junuh bends down to remove a pine needle near his ball and his ball rolls a half an inch. Only a young local boy named Hardy Greaves, who has been helping Bagger, has seen the ball move. The boy begs Junuh not to say anything. "Only you and me seen it, and I won't tell a soul. Cross my heart. Ain't nobody gonna know," the boy pleads. "I will, Hardy," Junuh replies, "and so will you." And he calls over his competitors and the match official to assess the one-stroke penalty on himself. The home crowd deflates. Even his competitors don't want it to go this way, but they are inspired by Junuh's integrity.

Once the penalty has been assessed, Bagger casually bids Junuh farewell. Everyone is shocked. The match still hangs in the balance. But Bagger knows his work has been completed. Now left to his own devices, Junuh reaches the green safely and sinks an improbable 30-foot putt to seal the unforgettable match in a tie. Bagger hears the crowd in the distance explode in cheers and he smiles and dances a little jig. He knows that in giving Rannulph Junuh his authentic swing back, he has taught him the incomparable value of attaching his best and truest self to his efforts.

———

When your grind is void of personal purpose it produces sparks that lack deep meaning and significance. Left unaddressed for too long, this sort of grinding eventually turns to concession. "It is what it is," we often say. In saying (or thinking) it, we are agreeing that work is, and will remain, void of the passion that transitions your days from transactional to transcendent. At its worse, this can look or at least feel like the character Rannulph Junuh—resolved that life just isn't very hopeful, isn't very promising. So the best course is to hole up in obscurity and do what we have to do to survive.

Trouble is, you are always capable of transcendence, every day.

You feel it deep down, that hope is still there, even when you've been ignoring it for years. Sometimes it takes being in a pressure cooker to rediscover ourselves as honestly as possible and finally decide to move forward and take an authentic swing at life.

I was a lot like Rannulph Junuh. Although I hadn't lost myself amid the harshness and tragedy of war, I had lost myself in the trenches of corporate life. I was so deep in that I couldn't see my true colors or the full field of opportunities before me. Sadly, if I'd remained successful I probably would have continued undaunted in my ways indefinitely (it scares me to think for how long). Fortunately, I reached a breaking point around my third decade of life. Or, more accurately, I was broken. I lost all but my family. And like Junuh, I was pissed off. I didn't know what the point of those years had been.

Also like Junuh, I had a Bagger Vance. For me, it was painting. Through an introduction and my eventual immersion, I began to renew hope for myself, in myself. As I studied how the masters painted, and how Rembrandt was different from van Gogh and Picasso, I began to see differently. Not only did I see potential and opportunity in a way I'd never noticed before, I began to feel a new sense of responsibility—responsibility to myself—to discover and be who I am, not just who might make me successful. I started to breathe again. I could sleep again—until this deep dive into the who and whats and whys inside me stirred up a boiling idea that kept me up all night long.

I slipped out of bed on this night and walked to the kitchen, where I pulled out my idea file, this large manila folder I'd kept for years with a hodgepodge of intel and inspiration. None of it had an end goal in mind—at least I hadn't thought so to that point. In truth, the random scraps were sparks that I had never had the courage to pursue. There might be a quote from a movie, or an article that inspired me, or notes I'd scribbled down about Denny Dent, whom I'd seen perform when I was a student at the University of San Diego. Dent would crank up the Stones, throw paint on the canvas, and all of a sudden it was Mick Jagger. Or John Lennon. Or Hendrix. He'd crank out these portraits in minutes. I'd always been captivated by street artists, guys who would dish up moonscapes using spray paint and nothing more than pots and pans. Artists who didn't do the traditional gig but still created captivating pieces. I spread out the contents of the file on the kitchen table and started to play with the combinations of notes and scraps as if they were Legos.

Ideas spilled out during this long frenetic night. I jotted them down on napkins and stray papers. It was wild. It felt like something or someone was pulling me forward. As if I were just a passenger whose job was to take it all in and try to make sense of it.

By sunrise I was still scribbling, and my notes were all over the kitchen floor. That's when it dawned on me that I didn't have to throw away my knowledge on professional speaking and the marketing of it. I thought, *What if I could lasso some of these ideas bouncing around in my head and then channel them into an art form like Denny Dent's?* Present a breakthrough approach to a subject using a medium so engaging that the audience wouldn't realize they'd just experienced a keynote? It was not art or commerce. It was art and business: thinking expansively like an artist, and then contracting and executing like an entrepreneur. Delivering action-able content like a speaker and entertaining like a live musician. Using different channels of interaction to activate an audience and moving them from passive consumers into engaged participants.

In the morning, Tasha came down and asked why I never came to bed. "I think I've figured it out," I answered. "What I want to do with my life."

Of course, at that point it was really just another crazy dream. But this one drove me to work my ass off. The spark—a true spark from inside me—drove me to grind. It felt more attached to me, more like the work I was meant to do than anything I'd done before. I was a fool in love. I would do anything to learn, anything to grow, any-thing to become great and make this thing in my head a reality. I'd found a spark that compelled me to grind. No, not just compelled me; I was giddy to grind.

And so I began grinding. The sparks continued to fly and here I am now, more than fourteen years later, still in love with this grind. I finally realized that my grind was raising sparks all along; I was just ignoring them. Once I was free to embrace a fully fluid creative process, the value of those sparks suddenly glowed to life and I added them to the fire—especially sparks like my deep knowledge of the speaking industry and the folder full of inspiration. I saw that the ashes of my career and business contained the embers of an ex-citing future.

Today I'm living that future and it still sparks new ideas. My grind is just as flammable. And I'm more in love with it all than when I started. It's taken on new and deeper meaning the more I've found myself in it. That's when you know who you are is attached to what you do.

———

When Michka Assayas asked Bono what initially set U2 apart from all the other great bands of the 1980s, the inimitable front man said, "The spark. There was something original about our point of view, even if it wasn't very well expressed. And we were relentless. Just those two things can get you places."

You can paint by the numbers, but your products will lack the very thing that's essential to art that moves not just others but the one who created it. Winston Churchill called courage the primary human quality because it guarantees all others. It takes courage to attach yourself to your work, especially if you've lost yourself along the way. But it's worth it. Not just in the end but today, the day you begin.

Don't aim for balance. Don't buy into detachment. Take courage and aim for integration—the folding of all you are into what you do. The word "courage" comes from the Old French word *cuer*, which originated from the Latin word *cor*, which means "heart." It takes all your heart to put yourself out there in the world. But nothing else is more yours to give. What you have is enough, especially when it's true. "We are each," writes Natalie Goldberg, "a concert reverberating with our whole lives and reflecting and amplifying the world around us."

Don't be afraid to turn up your volume.

3

KEEP YOUR DAY JOB

Instead of picking your career and backfilling your life behind that, what if you pick your life and backfill your career with whatever is left over?

—Bob Goff

HAVE YOU BEEN TELLING YOURSELF THE TRUTH? HAVE you been offering your whole self to the roles in your life?

This is certainly no indictment of your character. If that were the case, I'd be at the top of the list of suspects. We're not talking about dishonesty. We're talking about doing life, creating daily, from your whole self, which must include your heart.

Many of us have been doing life from our heads. The irony is that the logical path often causes us more confusion than clarity. "No man," wrote Nathaniel Hawthorne in *The Scarlet Letter,* "for any considerable period, can wear one face to himself and another to the multitude, without finally getting bewildered as to which may be the true."

Prior to speaking and performing for a living, I took a logical, linear approach to work. My dad's example proved to me that if you put your mind to something and do the work, you can accomplish anything. While there's some truth to that, it's a trap if your heart's never in it, too.

To do only what makes sense is the choice of a people without choices, a people with little if any freedoms. If you live in America or many other parts of the world, that's not you. You have more choices than you can count and the freedom to explore them to your heart's content. One of the most important choices you will make in life is to explore where you are right now, in the job you currently possess, within the relationships you currently have, at the places you regularly visit. Within your current context lies more creative opportunities than you probably ever realized. There are no dead-end streets for the truly creative.

To grind your sparks and spark your grind . . .
KEEP YOUR DAY JOB

As Edgar Lee Masters concludes in *Spoon River Anthology:*

To put meaning in one's life may end in madness,
But life without meaning is the torture
Of restlessness and vague desire—
It is a boat longing for the sea and yet afraid.

Being a constant creator begins by unlocking what is in your heart, right here, right now. You might have been playing that role for such a long time that it seems absurd to think you could actually do something different, something truly creative and heartfelt. But there is no question you can. Because as this change occurs inside you, it changes the appearance of the world around you. Yes, this is true even for a job you consider far from your heart.

The infusion of your whole self into any environment in which you find yourself will change how you see that environment.

To this day I still marvel that there were regular hints—sparks I'd continually tucked away—that were trying to converge and ignite a fire in me that was so close to what I already did. But now I speak instead of representing people who speak, and promote my own authentic brand and passions rather than others'.

Although I was forced out of my day job, I'd much rather have uncovered my creative potential without that heartache, stress, and utter embarrassment. I'm going to assume you feel the same. Don't buy the notion that you have to journey beyond your current context to find the greater creativity you're looking for. Greater creative potential is within you, in your whole self. Therein lies your power. Don't go looking for another field until you've taken an authentic swing where you are.

There are four reasons why your current roles are the best place to begin grinding new sparks:

Reason one: Your current roles are your reality.

I find that many a dreamer is prone to undervalue and even

neglect his reality in favor of future hope and wonder. But escaping one's current roles—even if only in a mental or emotional way—is a much more painful and potentially catastrophic move than learning to see them in a different light and approach them with a more creative hand.

A common mistake many hard-core Igniters make is that they are too quick to condemn the present. They believe that if an idea isn't easy to apply or widely accepted in their current circumstances, the circumstances are the problem. Instead of embedding themselves deeply and grinding out their circumstances, many Igniters simply look for new circumstances. This was the modus operandi of the artists I met in Southern California in my early days of immersion into the art world. They felt that the world in which they lived—including the friends and family around them, their instructors, their cities, their churches, the owners of the businesses they visited, and the fellow customers visiting those businesses—just didn't get it, just didn't understand or appreciate the importance of their creations. They would begin to withdraw, they became self-absorbed and sometimes even depressed. They involuntarily started to migrate toward fulfilling the cliché of the "starving artist." "Why didn't the world understand their creations?" they'd ask.

They liked to point to van Gogh, who received very little recognition while alive, as their proof that this sort of misunderstanding happens often with very creative people.

The fact is, van Gogh is the exception. Especially in today's hyperconnected world.

If you've something inventive to offer and you can't find an audience, the issue is usually the offering or the offerer, not the audience. It's usually a problem of either being detached from who you are or detached from where you are. That means that either your creations aren't original, or they aren't relevant. Sometimes it's both.

Whether you're an Igniter or a Grinder, embrace your current reality because, frankly, it's the only reality you have. This doesn't mean you have to like it. It also doesn't mean you have to accept it as it is. Many realities throughout history needed to change; they desperately needed a creator to come in and not only envision a new reality but begin digging the foundation with his or her own hands. This sort of change never happens from a detached stance. It always happens when creators dive headfirst and heartfirst into their current realities and dirty their hands.

This brings up the second reason why keeping your day job—or embracing your current roles—is where you should begin creating.

Reason two: Your current roles are the most prime real estate available to you for introducing creative solutions.

From Joan of Arc, Martin Luther, and William Wilberforce, to Gandhi, Martin Luther King Jr., and Nelson Mandela, many of history's greatest artists were simply common people who immersed themselves in their current roles and realities. They didn't brush them off or consider them out of touch with their personal ideas. They did the opposite. They remained where they were, sought to fully understand their contexts, and then infected them with groundbreaking ideas and creations, not in a contrived effort at vainglory but because their realities needed a way forward.

On refusing England's imperialism in France, the teenage peasant girl Joan of Arc supposedly asserted that "to sacrifice what you are and to live without belief, that is a fate more terrible than dying."

Of his Ninety-five Theses indicting the Roman Catholic Church for ungodly behavior, the German monk Martin Luther confessed, "I cannot do otherwise."

In response to the harsh opposition to his antislavery stance in England, the statesman William Wilberforce proclaimed, "If to be feelingly alive to the sufferings of my fellow-creatures and to be warmed with the desire of relieving their distresses is to be a fanatic, I am one of the most incurable fanatics ever permitted to be at large."

An impoverished but no less diminished Mahatma Gandhi maintained that "a 'No' uttered from the deepest conviction is better than a 'Yes' merely uttered to please, or worse, to avoid trouble."

The man who pushed America toward racial equality, Martin Luther King Jr., declared, "A man who won't die for something is not fit to live."

And the leader who became a prisoner to free his country from bigotry, Nelson Mandela avowed, "There is no passion to be found playing small."

While history does not categorize them as artists, all were creators of the highest form because their words and actions painted a new and better reality. Their canvases were the inert circumstances in which they lived. Their creations were the changes their circumstances needed.

They were artists not because they produced a piece of music or a colored canvas to entertain the masses. They were artists because they had the courage to challenge the flawed and unsatisfactory mores of their day and take groundbreaking action to improve them.

Although the results of their art changed the course of history, the nature of their circumstances is not unfamiliar to you or me. All found themselves in the midst of conditions that were not all they could or should be. While they could not change the history that brought about the deficiencies, they could control the way forward as much as one individual was able, which is more than many of us realize. All believed they had a say in the solution. And they did something you and I can do any time we are faced with a challenge or problem or unsatisfactory situation. They ground their way to a resolution rather than leaving their post or sitting idly by and hoping for innovation to arrive through someone else.

I realize you might be someone who finds himself or herself in a particular circumstance that might seem impossible to improve, even if da Vinci himself was brought in to create the solution. Still, withhold your judgment until you're all in. The view changes when you're fully immersed and begin to truly grind. One small fire can illuminate a cave. New creative opportunities come into view, new ideas arise, and new emotions begin to surface. This is true whether your circumstances are bad or good.

Sparks, even small ones, can point us in a better way no matter where we are today. Sometimes they provide light to show us a new way. Sometimes they provide heat to inspire us to move.

My friend Grant, the writer I mentioned earlier who has produced more than fifty books—he was on a path to medical school in college. If you know anything about that path, you understand that you can't go at it half-assed. Either you're all in or you don't survive. Grant was one of the all-in guys. Not only was he in the premed program, he also worked twenty hours a week for the marketing department of a large local hospital as a means of learning the industry.

Three years into college, Grant was locked in and on his way. There's another piece of this story that sweetened his path. His grandfather was a beloved physician in Southern California. He was a general practitioner of the olden days—delivered babies, performed surgeries, did house calls until the day he retired. His community respected him as a man of the "Greatest Generation": he had served his country in World War II, then came home and served his community. And this was the red carpet that was rolled out in front of my friend: his grandfather planned to retire after he finished medical school and hand the practice over to him. The practice housed files on more than thirteen thousand patients. It was a compelling reason to grind even if his heart wasn't in it. But it was.

Then a spark that changed his reality rose in the second semester of Grant's third year of college.

He was taking the speech class that all students of his college were required to take, regardless of their majors. The first assignment was to write a speech about a life experience, and the professor, as a means of easing students into giving speeches before the large class, allowed her students to read their first speech rather than recite it from memory. The following week, when the professor asked for volunteers to give their speeches, Grant raised his hand first and read a story he'd written about his life thus far. What happened soon thereafter was completely unexpected.

The class concluded and he packed up his things and headed for the door. That's where his professor stopped him to ask if he'd ever had anything published.

Grant laughed as he shook his head.

"You have a gift," the professor said. "I think you should take a creative writing class."

Grant didn't know what to do with the suggestion, but he thanked his professor and promised to consider it. That evening he reviewed his remaining course load for his final two semesters and it turned out he had one elective class left to fill. He decided to pursue that creative writing class. Why not?

The adjunct professor of that class echoed the speech teacher's comments and encouraged Grant to lean into his raw talent. He did—all the while applying to medical schools and fielding the schools' responses. He began to write—in class and at home and whenever a thought came to him—and the more he wrote, the more he fell in love with writing.

Eventually, Grant decided to forgo medical school and stay in undergrad for another two years to study and practice writing. It was a big risk to grind this spark and to pursue a path that was mostly filled with unknowns, except one: he knew he loved to write. After graduation, Grant took a job traveling with an up-and-coming thought leader who was speaking more than a hundred times a year to audiences across the nation. His job was to know the man's products—the videos, books, and audio available for sale. There were, at the time, about fifty of them. He kept grinding. He watched, read, and listened to everything more than once, and kept up to date on new offerings as they were produced. Two years into the position, Grant was the go-to guy when anyone anywhere wanted to know what particular product would best suit an individual's or company's particular needs. It wasn't where he imagined himself when he made the decision not to pursue a career in medicine. But he knew he was making the most of his current reality. Grinding it out to see if the spark could grow. Then it did.

On a plane one evening, flying home from a speaking gig with the team and his boss, Grant was reading a book when the man he worked for approached him and mentioned he'd noticed how much he liked to read. "Do you read to learn or just for enjoyment?" asked the boss.

"I guess I read," Grant replied, "because I like to write."

"I didn't know you liked to write!" the boss bubbled. "I have a printed copy of a chapter from the next book I'm working on at my seat. Would you mind giving me your feedback?"

Grant obliged and wrote a few notes in the margins of the printout.

A week later he received a call from his boss's writing partner. "He's been looking for a second writer for six months," the writer explained. "He read your feedback and he believes you're it."

One month later Grant was welcomed into his new position as the thought leader's second writer. The first three books he and the senior writer produced were *New York Times* best sellers that have together sold more than five million copies. The timing of all this wasn't lost on my friend, who noted that the month in which he received news that the third book had become a *New York Times* best seller was the same month that he would have graduated from medical school. He ground a brighter spark and it lit a blaze that has allowed him to consult, write for, and collaborate with dozens of thought leaders, athletes, entrepreneurs, and celebrities over the last seventeen years.

What's important for you to see is that Grant had been preparing for that opportunity since forgoing medical school, but not in any sort of formal, scripted way. He didn't try to figure it all out before he moved. He also didn't sit back and wait for something big to come along. He simply stepped wholly into his reality, whatever that was, and ground it out with whatever he had to offer. In doing so, he took neither the safest route—which probably would have been waiting tables and trying to publish the great American novel—nor the most practical route into his grandfather's medical practice. He took the route that creators take, the route that takes into account both head and heart, the route that is often illuminated one spark at a time. He ground out each one until another promising spark appeared and ignited a new or better way.

Popular social media strategist Amy Jo Martin did something similar. She worked for the NBA's Phoenix Suns franchise as the director of digital media from 2005 to 2009, when the social media frontier was entirely new ground.

Amy Jo's job, as explicitly stated by the Suns' top brass, was to promote the team's brand, not the players' personal brands. (This sounds almost silly now, knowing how critical superstars are to their teams' brands, but, again, it was a new world back then.) Of course, Amy Jo was a renegade—as she explains in her book about this experience, *Renegades Write the Rules*—who didn't listen too well to the management. That's not entirely true, though; Amy Jo listened enough to keep her job. But the more the Suns' players asked her for help, the more she helped—behind the scenes.

She was one of the early pioneers who saw the immense value that social media could provide in humanizing a big corporate brand for its consumer audience. She saw that when Suns' superstars like Shaquille O'Neal and Steve Nash connected with fans in an authentic and personal way, this could only boost the brand of the Phoenix Suns. She was right, though the Suns' brass didn't see it at that time. But instead of resenting her bosses' mandate, she ground hard for nearly a year to prove them wrong for their own benefit, both above ground through creations like the first ever tweetup, and below their radar by implementing clever strategies for the players to grow their personal brands.

In that context, one particular spark kept flying: the players' brands were more potent than the corporate brand because they were able to build a more natural person-to-person interaction. Keep in mind, this was in 2007 and 2008. Few were the possibilities of social media communities. But Amy Jo leaned into the idea long enough to prove its fire would burn hot. Eventually, it became clear it was time to let the fire spread.

When Amy Jo's hand was slapped once again for helping Shaquille strategize ways to connect with and entertain what was then a hundred thousand followers, she knew it was time to start building out her idea full time. She put in her notice with the Suns and took on Shaq as her first client. Other clients came quickly, and in a matter of a few years she'd already fanned the initial spark into a blaze called Digital Royalty with individual clients like Dwayne "The Rock" Johnson and major corporate clients like Nike, Hilton Worldwide, and the Ultimate Fighting Championship (UFC). Approximately six years later, and still in her thirties, Amy Jo exited the profitable company to begin stoking new sparks. She's now watching closely to see which ones burn hot.

By grinding your present circumstances as Grant and Amy Jo did, you will create sparks you never imagined before. New frontiers will open up that you could not have brainstormed if you spent a month with a whiteboard. It's far easier to create sparks from the roles you're already in and the realities you know than trying to create sparks for roles you don't know firsthand and realities you don't understand.

Grind where you are, with what you have. This is where your best sparks often lie. Noticing them requires a combination of intellect and intuition. This is why you must be fully there—head and heart both in it.

Contrary to what some think, these two tools that emerge from your head and your heart—intellect and intuition—are not set in opposition to each other. In fact, learning to use them as allies keeps you in a constantly creative state.

Intellect without intuition is a smart person with little creative impact. Intuition without intellect is a spontaneous person with little creative progress. Grinders like intellect. Igniters like intuition. Both are necessary to ensure you don't miss seeing a spark where you are (like Grant's love of writing), or fail to capitalize on your current grind (like his traveling job).

Like a compass, intuition can keep you on course. But intuition doesn't always explain why or tell you precisely how to proceed. It's a feeling inside, a spiritual guideline of a sort. And it's not as unstable as it sounds. Malcolm Gladwell calls intuition a "body of submerged knowledge"—the stuff we don't even know that we've gleaned over the years through experience. This submerged knowledge comes out in the form of gut feelings and sudden insights, and giving them a voice is necessary if you want to capture sparks wherever you are.

You have a body of submerged knowledge right now that can offer you creative insights about the roles and realities before you. Use it to capture the sparks that arise from your current grind. Instability will surface when you begin reaching beyond your intuition. In other words, when you try to project your creativity onto roles and realities with which you have little experience. While it's great to dream, the most trustworthy sparks are all around you. They are not "out there." And even if you dream of another day in another place, you still have to blaze the trail there.

Speaking of bigger dreams beyond your current realities . . .

Reason three: Your current roles give you the needed support to take creative risks.

When you grind where you are, you do more than ignite legitimate sparks; you also provide a financial and emotional foundation from which you can pursue less certain creative ventures that might not pay right away, or maybe not ever—except through a greater measure of fulfillment, camaraderie, or purpose. Consider this important reality before you haul off and dump a paying gig in favor of a creative dream. Your day job pays the bills. That's no small thing.

Having to be creative to pay your mortgage is a difficult gig to sustain out of the gate. Without the bills paid, there will always be the temptation to shortchange your products if they're good enough to garner payment but not good enough to captivate a wide audience. You will also find it a challenge to choose a dream project with low compensation over a well-paying project that doesn't excite you. The beauty of not having to worry about money is that you are free to grind the wilder sparks inside you; you're free to sculpt even the most obscure creations. Neither your frontiers to explore nor your pace of creation is limited by earning an income or by the expectations of others. When monthly living is paid for, you are free to wander the outside edges of your creative potential without pressure.

"I love teaching," writes Thomas Bradshaw, an assistant communications professor at Northwestern University who is also a successful playwright and screenwriter, most recently for HBO/Harpo Films. "But having a job that doesn't get in the way of my writing also gives me another benefit: artistic freedom. I can choose to focus on projects that interest me instead of being forced to take every job that comes along because I need the money."

It comes down to your tolerance for uncertainty, explains

Bradshaw. The more certainty you have, particularly financial certainty, the more freedom you will feel to grind out the sparks that truly interest you. This stability is not a benefit that only a handful of creators have discovered. Nor is it a benefit that only aspiring or small-time creators enjoy. For decades, many of the world's greatest creators have enjoyed it.

This stands in contrast to the oft referenced—and perhaps just as oft caricatured—wild living of artists like Oscar Wilde or Ernest Hemingway. Wallace Stevens used his daily walks to his job—as an insurance salesman for the Hartford Accident and Indemnity Company—to inspire his Pulitzer Prize–winning poetry. Kurt Vonnegut managed a Saab dealership after the publication of his first novel, *Player Piano*. American poet William Carlos Williams used his prescription pads to write poetry while serving as the chief of pediatrics at Passaic General Hospital in Passaic, New Jersey, from 1924 until his death in 1963.

Of course, you don't have to keep your day job. No one is forcing you. You could join the ranks of starving artists who prefer to live on instant ramen and cheap coffee as you try to bring to life that game-changing idea or creation. But consider this reality if that is how you lean: according to Juri Koll, a filmmaker from Los Angeles and the cofounder of the Venice Institute of Contemporary Art, "In the United States there are about 115,000 young people who graduate from college with art degrees every year ... [and] at least another million early-to-mid career artists on the market. . . . If each of [the 6,500] galleries and dealers were willing and able to handle another two artists every year, it would still paint a pretty dismal picture of an artist's chance of getting noticed."

This isn't just the case for contemporary artists. How many sculptors do you know who are raking in the cash? Okay, let's be more current. How many freelance photographers do you know who are able to fully support themselves with the proceeds they receive from their work? How many writers? Better yet, how many bloggers?

When it comes to success as a creator, we often put on our dunce caps and point to the exceptions and call them the expectation. Or we just tap out. The reality of being a constant creator—especially as you first embrace this life—is that you can use all the support you can get. Financial support is at the top of the list. The support of family and friends is great, too, but let's be honest—those who love us the most aren't always the most objective art critics. Stick with securing a financial foundation and then be grateful you have people around you who will love you even though your first attempt at a watercolor painting looks like the tablecloth after a kids' ice-cream party.

A recent AOL Finance article asks, "How are you supposed to get anything done when you can barely afford a sandwich? . . . Even if you think you're the next [Pulitzer Prize–winning author and MIT professor] Junot Díaz, you're still going to have to pay your electric bill somehow, which means that sooner or later—probably sooner—you'll need to get a day job."

If you already have one, keep it. To begin, at least.

The AOL article goes on to profile six creatives who hold day jobs while simultaneously churning out creations beyond their nine-to-five responsibilities. One is Summer Pierre, a cartoonist, illustrator, and author of *The Artist in the Office*.

"Jobs and kids give artists a life," she says, "something so essential and yet underestimated for artists." In other words, if all you did was stare at the blank page every day, as Thomas Bradshaw says, you risk losing the very connection you have to real life and real emotions experienced by real people around you—the people who are, by the way, the same ones you hope will take an interest in your creations.

In a 2001 article for *The Guardian*, John O'Mahoney shared a humorous story about influential composer Philip Glass. Throughout his career as a celebrated music maker, Glass continued to work as both a taxi driver and plumber, which he felt kept him grounded in the real world. On one occasion, Glass was called to install a dishwasher in a SoHo home. Glass explained to O'Mahoney: "While working, I suddenly heard a noise and looked up to find Robert Hughes, the art critic of *Time* magazine, staring at me in disbelief. 'But you're Philip Glass! What are you doing here?' It was obvious that I was installing his dishwasher and I told him I would soon be finished. 'But you are an artist,' he protested. I explained that I was an artist but that I was sometimes a plumber as well and that he should go away and let me finish."

This connectedness is a critical point. Don't underestimate it. The more connected you are to the world in which you live through a day job, the more creative freedom you will have, the more creative material you will have to draw from, and the better understanding you will acquire about your viewing audience.

This brings up the final reason you should stick with your current work situation for now.

Reason four: When you simultaneously grind your current roles and your creative frontiers, you cultivate a symbiotic relationship that fuels both your day job and your creative potential.

Time has a lot to do with this. When you have fewer hours to grind your wilder sparks, your mind is forced to be more focused. While most Grinders have a built-in mechanism that naturally generates this healthy tension, Igniters tend not to. They prefer instead to explore without deadlines and expectations. The limited time each day is a good thing for Igniters who find it a challenge to start grinding some of those ideas.

But, let's be real here: we all need a little squeeze from time to time—especially for those creations we really want to see come to fruition. "I find that having a job is one of the best things in the world that could happen to me," confessed the beloved poet Wallace Stevens, who also held a career as an insurance executive. "It introduces discipline and regularity into one's life."

The flip side of the symbiotic relationship is that the self-discipline that's needed to be a good employee who shows up on time and carries out his responsibilities will seep back into your creative exploration when you're not sparking and grinding for a paycheck. In short, your good habits at work tend to carry over into other responsibilities and activities, including your currently unpaid creations.

While I've been using the phrase "day job" liberally to this point, a critical key to constant creativity is not to compartmentalize your life as your day job, and your passions, and your potential, and whatever else you might add into the equation. It's not this and that and the other thing. It's just this. It's just who you are and what you do. Your life is not a bingo game where you're constantly waiting for the next call, hoping it's your number. Your life is a puzzle with every piece already at your disposal. You just need the vision to see how all the pieces fit together. When you do that every day, sparks fly from every angle of your life.

Adopting this broader perspective requires what Maltese physician and psychologist Edward de Bono named lateral thinking.

De Bono maintains that when it comes to creativity, we are largely taught to think either vertically, which is straight-line, connect-the-dots critical thinking, or horizontally, which is basically vomiting ideas with no plans to implement them. Lateral thinking, instead, is thinking in terms of movement, considering how each idea and piece of information moves the whole forward, how the intel you take in improves your progress multilaterally, in every aspect of your circumstances. The goal of lateral thinking, says de Bono, is creation that is simple and effective.

Author Glenn Llopis, the son of Cuban immigrants who fled their motherland during Castro's revolution, uses the term "circular vision" to describe a primary catalyst that fuels lateral thinking. In his insightful book *Earning Serendipity,* he explains that witnessing his father's uncanny ability to remain constantly creative and opportunistic throughout his life taught him that innovation starts with how we see. "There is a reason we call the United States 'the land of opportunity,' but it is the immigrant who knows this better than anyone. He comes to America with nothing but faith, hope, and love, and he consequently views everything as opportunity. He is neither myopic nor careless in his pursuits but rather sees every relationship, every job, every dollar, and every day through the lens of potential. He thus sows entrepreneurial seeds wherever he goes— in people, in jobs, in new ventures, and experiences. . . . Some of his seeds sprout. . . . He cultivates these seeds through focus to ensure they grow to their potential. All the while, he continues sowing other seeds everywhere he goes."

In time, continues Llopis, this holistic opportunist begins to see fruit springing up in multiple areas of his life. We might call it luck, "had we no knowledge of the man's habits." Llopis's father, Francisco "Frank" Llopis, was the obvious inspiration for this description. Around the time he and his wife fled Cuba, Frank and his brother Manuel "Nolo" Llopis started a quartet with Leandro and Manolo Vegas called Los Llopis that became one of the preeminent bands of the 1960s in Spanish-speaking countries. Based in Argentina, they introduced the music world to the pachanga genre and were the first to mix American rock and roll with Afro-Antillean rhythms. When Frank Llopis finished playing music around his fortieth birthday, he brought his family from Buenos Aires to the United States. He went on to study chemical engineering at Columbia University and shortly thereafter was instrumental in the creation of Miller Lite. This string of creative pursuits continued until the year he died. In his nineties, Frank Llopis was still learning at least five new songs on his guitar each year.

While the life of Llopis's immigrant father makes a good case for a broader perspective on our lives, history furthers the case. Llopis bids us to consider iconic sparks like naval officer Richard James's discovery of the Slinky when a torsion spring fell from a worktable, and 3M chemist Patsy Sherman's discovery of Scotchgard when she spilled a liquid rubber compound on her shoe. These well-known sparks were generated and ground out by regular people who were neither hyperfocused nor dismissive about the contexts of their work. They were working "day jobs" and yet these jobs were treated like their laboratories of invention, discovery, and creativity.

"Opportunities are everywhere," Llopis points out. "But few have eyes to see." Those who see broadly are constant creators. To ensure that this is true of you, to ensure that you are in a state of constant creativity wherever you are, especially where you spend eight to ten hours a day, you should not only see with broad vision, you should also think in terms of comprehensive progress.

Each day is a day to create. Period. Constant creators see life as simply as that. They do not see a day broken up into sessions like the old American labor movement's slogan, "Eight hours for work, eight hours for rest, eight hours for what we will." They don't agree with Canadian 1980s rock band Loverboy, who sang, "Everybody's working for the weekend." They see themselves, first and foremost, as creators. And they see their primary role as creating.

"A master in the art of living draws no sharp distinction between his work and his play . . ." wrote Lawrence Pearsall Jacks, author of *Education Through Recreation,* in 1932. "He hardly knows which is which. He simply pursues his vision of excellence through whatever he is doing and leaves others to determine whether he is working or playing. To himself he always seems to be doing both."

Draw no lines. Start where you are, doing what you do. Wake up each day and go to create.

4

EMBRACE A ROUTINE

Routine, in an intelligent man, is a sign of ambition.

—W. H. Auden

CREATIVES ARE GENERALLY THOUGHT OF AS ECCEN-tric people, odd birds whose capricious lives ebb and flow with their latest whims. They dress weirdly or drink too much or smoke too much or sleep with too many people and this is, we suppose, just how they cope with the originality flowing from their wild minds into the works of their hands.

While you'll get no argument from me that creatives are generally eccentric people in one way or another, this portrait of a creative person gives a false notion about the process of creativity. First, it's an anecdotal conclusion about creativity that is based on the buzz-worthy stories of creators throughout history. The problem with buzzworthy intel is that it's often hyperbole. And it's usually only half of the story. But even if an eccentric creator was as outlandish as the stories make him sound, there is one aspect of the constant creator's life that almost never gets coverage despite it being the one trait that unites him with every other highly creative person on the planet: his discipline.

This idea that great creatives embrace strict discipline seems antonymic to their characters. It's not sexy. It's not dramatic. It may even dull the theatrical polish we like to put on their lifestyles—or our own. But there's no doubt that constant creators have learned that strategic discipline is more essential than their vices and foibles will ever be.

To grind your sparks and spark your grind . . .
EMBRACE A ROUTINE

Discipline came natural to me as a Grinder. The more disciplined I was as a boy, the more I paid attention to detail, the more my father said, "Attaboy!"

My father had excelled through hard work and details. He was an All-American shortstop who wasn't a home-run hitter. As in the film *Moneyball*, he was the kind of guy Billy Bean sought out, who got on base as much as possible. He rarely struck out. He made contact nearly every at bat. He was highly productive. And all that hard work and attention to detail in sports translated into a rewarding life as a physician.

This was my primary model when I was a boy and so I emulated it not only in my schoolwork but in the sport I played throughout high school and college: wrestling. At practice, we'd often be asked to complete ten taxing drills in a row and you assumed that you were going to have to go to failure at each drill. I bought in and excelled. Weight lifting was a part of training so I started lifting. That also required discipline and grit. I was rewarded there, too. I started lifting more than others my age, competing and winning. Eating good food several times a day became part of my weight-lifting routine as well. I'd train twice a day and eat six times. I'd constantly read up on the latest fitness trends. Progress spoke to me. Routine made sense. When I went into the corporate world, I kept this up.

But there was a problem with my mental posture.

As I embraced routine in every aspect of my adult life, I became less and less aware of what else was around me: less aware of my external environment—especially more efficient, creative opportunities for progress and growth; and less aware of my internal environment—that place in my spirit that was asking for more than predictable destinations. As I've confessed, many sparks got missed along the way, which largely led not only to my corporate demise but also to my complete emptiness thereafter. The lesson I had to learn was how to be disciplined as a creator—as both a Grinder and an Igniter. There's a difference. To be disciplined as a creator requires a more mindful routine that allows for fast progress and simultaneous flexibility to explore without an immediate deadline.

After I lost my business and I immersed myself in the world of creatives and creations, I felt the natural pull to let go of all that might hinder me—career expectations, household chores, even obligations outside my family. Still, I knew enough to know I couldn't just float off into space and return to reality when it felt right. I knew nothing would get done and, besides, I felt the increasing pressure of eventually needing a paycheck. I was okay taking risks to figure things out quicker, but I knew we'd only last so long without anything coming in.

There was this damned-if-I-do, damned-if-I-don't scenario going on in my mind. I was floundering some. I knew I needed to open up and keep exploring and testing so I could discover the best way to roll out and monetize this new performing artist idea inside me. But I also knew I needed to make progress, and to make progress I needed to grind out a product, even if it was an imperfect prototype.

This pressure from both sides is where you will find yourself as you seek a more constant stream of creativity, and you should know it's a perfectly natural feeling initially. It's a good one, too, even if it doesn't feel that way right away.

In *Creativity*, Mihaly Csikszentmihalyi explains, "When people are asked to choose from a list the best description of how they feel when doing whatever they enjoy doing most . . . the answer most frequently chosen is 'designing or discovering something new.'" While this might seem strange at first, says Csikszentmihalyi, after further consideration it makes perfect sense.

Imagine, he continues, that you are creating a new life-form from scratch and you want it to have the best chance of survival in a complex and unpredictable environment (like the one we all live in now). How would you go about it? "You want to build into this organism some mechanism that will prepare it to confront as many of the sudden dangers and to take advantage of as many of the opportunities that arise as possible." How? According to Csikszentmihalyi, by making this organism driven to efficiency, it learns best practices and repeats them. It would also be rewarded for new creations and discoveries, whether or not they are immediately useful. Thus the new life-form can adapt and evolve according to new information and better ideas, heading off anything that could threatens its survival.

"This," says Csikszentmihalyi, "is what seems to have happened with our race. . . . We are generally torn between two opposite sets of instructions programmed into the brain: the least-effort imperative on one side, and the claims of creativity on the other." We have a nervous system that's torn between the rewards of conserving energy and of using it constructively. In other words, our nervous system is a two-timer, and you need to know when and with whom to let it cheat.

Csikszentmihalyi says the force of efficiency—which he also calls entropy or the urge to use our energy wisely—is stronger in most people than the urge to create. As he points out, this is a good thing. "If we didn't have this built-in regulator, we could easily kill ourselves by running ragged and then not having enough reserves of strength, body fat, or nervous energy to face the unexpected."

On the other hand, if we weren't also compelled to discover new ways of being and doing, we would stagnate as a species—and as individuals.

This is a creativity conundrum: we need to be efficient and use our energy wisely but in order to make progress we also need to explore, ideate, create.

Routine is the glue that holds them together.

Adventure, exploration, discovery . . . these activities require freedom of action and expression. It's the old axiom that you can't discover new lands without losing sight of the shore. It's true. To be creative, there has to be a constant willingness to let go—of assumptions, of current knowledge, of safety nets—and Igniters have a natural inclination to do this. But there must also be structure if you want to make any real strides in your creative efforts—not so much structure that your efforts are constantly unrefined, but enough to force you to take action and produce something, anything, on a daily basis.

I mentioned earlier in the book that Hemingway was very deliberate about nearly everything he did. Like me, he grew up with a disciplined physician as a father. This structure carried over into his first job after high school as a newspaper reporter for the *Kansas City Star,* where the deadlines came every week and he didn't have the luxury to wait until he felt like working. He then became a military man, enlisting as an ambulance driver in World War I. After the war, he returned to journalism as a foreign correspondent and lived with his first wife among the famous expat crowd in Paris that included Ezra Pound, Pablo Picasso, Gertrude Stein, and James Joyce.

Hemingway's life in Paris wasn't one that naturally bred structure like a newspaper gig did, but he nonetheless established a routine for his day, down to the smallest details. This kept him on top of his game and allowed him to produce. One of Hemingway's unique habits was always to leave off his writing at a place where he knew what was coming next. He'd rise before dawn and stop typing around 1:00 P.M., purposefully calling it a day when he had more writing in him. Why? He felt this ensured that when he came to write the next morning, he would not struggle to create momentum.

One additional rule he followed was to count the number of words he'd written each day and record that number on a board next to his typewriter. He felt this kept him honest and prohibited him from congratulating himself for making good progress when the numbers said he hadn't.

Then, once he'd deliberately left off his writing prematurely and recorded his word count, Hemingway headed to a local pub for lunch and drinks. Sometimes alone—in which case he'd study human nature all around him as research for his works—but often with friends on whom he could test out his ideas and his characters' emotions. Hemingway felt that a writer could only write what he knew to be true. And so he sought to learn as much as he possibly could about human nature in the places where people congregated most: pubs, cafés, and restaurants.

Within the strategic fences and freedom of this routine, Hemingway produced his first novel, *The Sun Also Rises*, which catapulted him into international fame as an author.

Hemingway knew well that creativity without structure is like a river without banks. You might have a flood of ideas every day, but with no structure to get them moving, your ideas end up bobbing in an ever-expanding puddle. Your progress is greatly limited to laps around the shallows.

Conversely, creativity within the right structure is like a river with banks. Ideas move faster in the current of your work and yet there is still room for them to deepen and even accelerate as needed by narrowing the banks.

I had to learn how to deploy this sort of structure when I began to let my inner Igniter breathe. As I've said, my compelling instinct was to let my ideas take me wherever they wanted because I had spent nearly a decade pounding in one nail at a time. But my inner monologue told me to be wary of falling prey to this approach again. Had I reacted according to my emotions, I would never have learned to perform the way I do on stage today.

To learn how to paint well and fast, I had to create an environment where daily I could both think freely and also take chances with immediate action, where I could toss an idea into the current of my daily grind and see if it would sink or swim. If one swam, I'd jump in with the idea and see how far I could take it before I had to take a breath or swim to the shore and evaluate my progress. The only way I could do this was to establish boundaries for not only my time and energy but my goals. I wouldn't just let myself get away with spending the day pondering, especially when I needed to construct a new income stream. While I certainly had to figure out what the art world had to offer me—or perhaps better said, what I had to offer it—I still made myself write down or type up ideas or, best of all, test them out. When I really thought I was onto something, I would immediately go to work and close in the riverbanks. This is what it took for me to learn to paint.

For instance, take a celebrity like Bono, one of my early subjects. When I painted him the first time, I worked almost the entire day to produce a photo-realistic portrait. Then I evaluated and studied it, and then went at it again, trying to knock it out in four hours. I repeated that same process until I was able to complete the painting in an hour, then thirty-six minutes, then fourteen minutes. It took me about three months to compress that painting down to a three-minute burst. When I was just getting started, I'd complete at least fifty iterations to master a three-minute speed painting. Without a commitment to that routine, I'd have nothing to perform. I doubt anyone would want to watch a guy paint for four hours.

But here's an important point about this routine. I learned to step back and assess my work and see how I could improve it, which in this particular case meant not only creating a more realistic picture but also creating one with fewer strokes of the paintbrush. By allowing for these strategic pan-out sessions after each painting was complete, I sparked an important technical innovation in my work.

I started out painting on a traditional white canvas, until I surmised that if I painted on a black canvas, I just had to pull the lights forward in the likeness of whatever I was painting. I could spend my time connecting the regions of light. Because the background was already black, the dark voids between my paint strokes would naturally create the contour and shadow. This was a small but critical idea that I began to test immediately.

The initial result was that I had to learn to paint in a slightly different manner, more reserved and careful, with strategically placed strokes that allowed the black backdrop to work for me and not against me. The change didn't appear to succeed immediately because of the time I needed to retrain my skills. If you looked at my time spent painting one canvas, it appeared I had backslidden. But I knew this new approach was a spark with promise, so I kept with the routine, producing a painting, then panning back out to study and evaluate, then grinding it out again. Within a year, I had mastered the new method of painting and I subsequently switched to all black canvases from that day forward.

It's one thing to embrace structure to get an idea in your head into a tangible form. It's an entirely different thing to take that tangible creation and mold it into something that is distinctive and memorable. Many creators get the product finished and then move on to the next product. That can be a mistake. Often, the initial product still contains some embers that just need a little more stoking to ignite a bigger flame.

The more I painted these black canvases, the quicker I could go from a first attempt of a likeness to a three-minute photo-realistic burst. What once took me three months to master eventually took me a week. My routine got me that far, but I knew there wasn't much about my skill that was truly distinct. There were other artists who could paint well and fast. I needed to continue improving in one way or another. So when I wasn't painting, my free time was spent studying with an art instructor I'll call Cynthia. She was one of the few who could teach me a style few painters ever attempt. I knew if I could pull it off, the experience I offered onstage would be perfect for an audience seeking a visceral experience of creativity. This novel method would keep them on the edge of their seats, completely unaware of what I was painting, and then gradually the strokes would build to a crescendo until finally I would flip the canvas and voila: "Holy crap, he just did a painting in three minutes—upside down!"

That became a big differentiator for me. Again, I ground out the spark with strict routine and went backward in my productivity for a season in order to master a method that would eventually move me further forward. I knew plenty of speakers on the circuit talked about creativity. But if I showed an audience creativity, not something that just registered in their heads but an experience that helped them truly feel the presence of creativity in their own bodies and minds, I knew I had something incredibly unique and memorable. Grinding out that spark with a rigorous and initially counterproductive routine turned into a steady fire that still burns today.

It is a passion of mine to make daily, breakthrough creativity accessible to everyone in a way that it was not to me when I needed it most. From experience I know this access can happen in an instant if I can awaken the creative spirit inside an individual. It's there—I know it is—in you, in me, in all of us. So I embrace it as one of my callings in life to say: you already have a resource built into your DNA that can solve your toughest problems, enrich the most important roles you play, and illuminate the potential of your life for as long as you're alive. As the passion to spread this message grew in my early days of performing, so, too, did my opportunities.

Within three years Tasha was booking a hundred shows a year for me, and my rates steadily increased. During that time, I still regularly tinkered with my routine until I found the one that kept me performing at a high level while allowing my presentation to continue evolving into more effective iterations.

This is an important point. Once I had created something and began selling it regularly—once I officially became a keynote speaker (meaning somebody paid me for it)—I became more and more comfortable with the routine of creating this particular product, especially as I locked into my sweet spot for learning new paintings and mastering them quickly. The risk of creating that product diminished over time. There was a growing temptation to just milk this creation as far as it could go in its current iteration. But being in the corporate world—especially in the world of professional speakers, where the next big one was a TED Talk away—I knew what I did would eventually grow stale. Others would model it. Someone would come along and do more. I wanted—I needed—to continue setting my creative work apart.

When you're at the point where a creation is working and working well, this is when your routine can either propel you further or pummel you.

If you find yourself in a steady river current that's moving along nicely with the routine you have in place, it can be all too easy to inflate a tube and enjoy the ride. But what happens to natural rivers happens to creative momentum as well. As seasons change and unpredictable environmental patterns occur, the current you're in can change. It can slow down. It can even dry up. This is what happens when you allow your routine to numb your desire for novelty, when you love routine for its ability to conserve your energy but forget its purpose in allowing you to use your energy constructively. It's like loving a person for what she does for you, but losing interest in what she alone can offer or what you can do together.

When your routine begins to work its magic, it's not time to revel in the conservation of your energy. Sure, celebrate. Stretch your hamstrings. Take a power nap. Then start using those stores of energy your routine has created to create more and better creations.

Start by looking at your "finished" creations from all angles. How can you improve them? What about them isn't particularly original? What about them isn't signature you?

One of the ways I integrate ongoing research into my routine is to attend local live shows, particularly when I'm traveling to new cities for keynote performances. It doesn't matter whether it's Madonna in Miami or Bruce Springsteen in Boston—I just want to see thriving performers doing their thing and then learn something from them.

I don't sit in the back row, either. If there is a mosh pit, I'm jumping in and getting thrashed around. I want to feel the heartbeat of the show and experience the dynamic relationship between performer and audience.

My ultimate goal with this element of my routine is to understand how and why these performers are successful at connecting with an audience. When and why do their crowds respond fanatically? The intel I acquire helps me continually improve my own performances. The context even reinforces the conserve-and-create mandates of a great routine.

While the top performers I observe plan strategic set lists ahead of time based on what songs their audience enjoys and what sort of show they want to put on, these performers allow themselves freedom to respond to the crowd's pulse. This helps them depart from the set list at opportune moments to create an even more engaging performance. I learned from this model and began applying it immediately. I transferred this awareness into every one of my performances. From the second I take the stage, I listen. I go in search of the silent rhythms that are unique to every audience and every different venue. I feel around for the heartbeat of the audience so I can align my speaking cadence with their breathing patterns, their thought processes, and how they are responding to my message in real time.

Today my preperformance routine starts the moment I am booked for a keynote. If the company is public, the very first thing I do is purchase a sizable portion of the stock. I want a pound of flesh in the game. This also helps me better understand their competitive landscape and potential pitfalls. I learn and perform differently when I am both financially and emotionally invested in the outcome.

From there, I'll start reading up on the company. I set my social media alerts to make me aware of what news events are moving the needle. I require every client to fill out an extensive preprogram questionnaire to give me specific insights about its organization. I'll schedule a conference call with representatives of the organization. I do not breeze through these calls. I do a deep dive, spending considerable time interviewing the executives and taking copious notes. I'm prodding them to feel their pain points and opportunities. I also spend time reviewing their financial reports, social media, their competitors and their brand in the market. Finally, I learn the words and language popular within the company. Whatever their terminology is, I assimilate it into my presentation.

From there, every performance is like a special ops mission. I pack up clothes, paint, and canvases, and ship them to each location. The canvases come in these cardboard boxes on which I've already stenciled celebrity portraits—when they arrive at the hotel a few days before the event, there's already this buzz building, this sense of mystery, this foreshadowing. Then I personally travel light. It's just me and my laptop on the plane. I don't travel with my producer because I'm a complete introvert. For the same reason, I don't do meet and greets or special dinners. I don't even network. I perform for sixty minutes, then disappear. For me, that's part of the discipline. To give my best possible performance, I have to be free of distractions before and after the show. The client doesn't even know when I arrive, because I need to spend that time quietly to prepare.

Sixty minutes before my performance, I meet with my show producer. He has already confirmed with the on-site production team to ensure flawless execution. He's like an aide-de-camp or a caddy, removing friction and clutter from my life before I perform. He frees me up in every aspect, allowing me to focus all my attention exclusively on being present for the audience. He anticipates challenges and removes them so I never see them. He knows what I need and how I need it. If I start communicating with technical production teams prior to my performance, it takes me off my game. So I don't. I am focused. I ramp up, preparing myself mentally, physically, and emotionally to ensure that I make an authentic connection with the audience.

There's no standard easel, so my producer often builds them. He and his team will use sandbags and gaffs and tape so the easel won't rock. They test the subwoofers and the lighting. I see very little of this. I'm on stage meditating, envisioning, entering into the moment I've been grinding for, the moment my routine has given me. Then we launch into it. We have gone to great lengths to create epic audience experiences beyond delivery of actionable content. We have hired and worked extensively with Cirque du Soleil show producers to enhance the aesthetics and show production for the audience. We are designing and testing creativity-geared technology that is way ahead of its time and has yet to see the marketplace. But this process of ideation begets new ideas on blurring the lines between lecture and rock show.

We have pushed boundaries and explored how the production experience is received from every seat, every set of eyes and ears in the audience, and how to use staging, lights, video, music, aesthetics, timing, cadence, humor, and hidden reveals to create aha! moments and special effects that connect the audience to the experience and trigger memorable emotional engagement.

When everything's firing, the show has both a dynamic and choreographed flow and it's a beautiful day. This is where the spark ignites and reignites for me every week.

But these sixty-minute sparks would never light without weeks and months of consistent routine. I am a free and creative spirit live from the stage, but I am a control freak with militaristic attention to detail to ensure precision and flawless execution prior to taking the stage. In truth, my routine of the past fourteen years has sparked the hour my audience sees today. And I hope it'll be fourteen years better fourteen years from now.

This is what it takes for me to remain in a state of constant creativity with my work. Without an ability to embrace my routine, I shudder to think where I'd be instead. But you should know that the ideal routine of one creator is rarely perfect for another. There is no one-size-fits-all approach to structuring your days to propel you into a daily current of creativity. Be willing to tinker some until you reach an honest understanding of what works best for you, in the moment in which you're living now. That moment will change, changing your opportunities. So find one routine whose core elements remain the same, thus allowing you to consistently use your energy efficiently and creatively.

———

In *Daily Rituals,* Mason Currey illustrates that there's little similarity between someone like French novelist Gustave Flaubert—a night owl who woke daily at 10:00 A.M. and banged on the ceiling to summon his mom for a chat—and the Swiss-French architect Le Corbusier, who shot up at 6:00 A.M. for forty-five minutes of exercise. "But they each did what they did with iron regularity," writes Oliver Burkeman of *The Guardian.* In his review of Currey's book, he references W. H. Auden's advice that creators must "Decide what you want or ought to do with the day, then always do it at exactly the same moment every day." Auden's reason? So that "passion will give you no trouble."

Immanuel Kant's neighbors, writes Burkeman, could set their clocks by his daily routine. While this seems like an "intimidating level of self-discipline," Burkeman rightly calls it a "safety net." However, this kind of safety isn't the security that we traditionally seek from a job or a large sum in the bank. It's the sort of safety that we feel when we know we're doing precisely what we need to be doing in order to both personalize and maximize our creative capacity.

All routine requires risk, especially at the outset. There's no way around it. So strap in when you're trying to establish yours. It won't feel efficient at first—much like my efforts to paint on a black canvas. When you begin, you're often in the dark about the outcome. You might feel the emotions one feels in the dark, both bad and good: impatience, confusion, frustration . . . hope, excitement, wonder. Stick it out. As your mind, body, and spirit conform to the regularity of a routine, certain things that once took effort become involuntary.

The psychologist and philosopher William James claimed that by making as many aspects of our lives as automatic as possible, we could "free our minds to advance to really interesting fields of action." When he said this in the late 1800s, there was little to prove the assertion. Today, as journalist Daniel Coyle points out in his book *The Talent Code,* scientists now believe that each time we perform a task, the specific neurons that fired to make the task possible grow a layer of fatty tissue around them called myelin, which serves as an insulator so these same neurons can fire more efficiently the next time they're needed. Essentially, this means that the more you repeat the same activity, the more its specific neurons are insulated, the more efficient and automatic the activity becomes.

Since the 1980s we've gone round and round about whether having too much on our minds is good or bad for us but there is one

thing most experts can agree on: the more activities we can auto-
mate and carry out by habit, the freer our minds are to accommo-
date and properly filter the new ideas and information constantly
swirling around us. This is why, when he was in office, President Barak
Obama routinely wore suits in the same two colors.

"You'll see I wear only gray or blue suits," Obama told Michael
Lewis in a 2012 article for *Vanity Fair.* "I'm trying to pare down
decisions. I don't want to make decisions about what I'm eating or
wearing. Because I have too many other decisions to make. You need
to focus your decision-making energy. You need to routinize yourself. . . . You can't be going through the day distracted by trivia."

But beware that you can take this too far. Obama confessed to
Lewis that the level to which he had to be "routinized" as the president of the United States is unnatural. With too much under routine,
"You can't wander around. It's much harder to be surprised. You
don't have those moments of serendipity."

When your creative urge begins to diminish, when you no longer have the space to wander both mentally and physically, you've
taken your routine too far, spread it too broadly. Back off and build
in some more margin. But no matter how much tinkering it takes to
find your groove, don't give up. With no routine at all, you will never
touch your creative potential.

On one hand, creativity can reach anything in our lives. But
the reality is that some of us don't care to dress more creatively, for
instance (Steve Jobs was a prime example). But we all have roles
and activities in our lives that really matter, and those are different
for everyone. When I say you must establish your routine, I am

specifically talking about freeing up space to be more creative in the areas of your life that matter most. That requires two parts: streamlining activities that matter less (perhaps like your clothing), and routinizing activities in your life that matter most, so that you have space and time to grow, to spark and grind.

There's a very simple reason we tend to have big ideas on vacation. Much of what isn't significant is removed. And what is significant is with us full time. In effect, vacations impose a new routine on us that opens us up to great possibilities in the areas that matter most. In our hearts, we know what these are. When we get these right and experience the rewards of creativity there, new frontiers are clearer rather than capricious, and we can have confidence entering them. In truth, our priorities are always frontiers each day, filled with mystery, possibility, and surprising joy. We just must free up time to enter them.

It's not easy at first; but few efforts are more worth your energy. Sadly, the battle to establish a quality routine takes out many would-be creators every year. Countless aspiring writers started with big ideas and then never finished their books. Photographers dropped a couple of grand on nice equipment and then never learned how to use half the functions. Entrepreneurs clinked glasses upon receiving an investment and then cashed in their chips before seeing their businesses thrive. To commit to anything that promises novelty is usually exciting. But when it doesn't deliver right away, we tend to back into our creature comforts. Resist this urge.

Resist the urge to coast when the routine is working. And resist the urge to give up trying to establish yours when it's challenging to find your stride.

When you shy away from a routine that fosters both efficiency and creativity, what you're really running from is risk. Creating anything is risky. And eliminating trivial tasks and automating others can feel unnatural. But the good news is that when you find your groove, the more you rely on it the less risky it feels.

This is something adventure athletes like BASE jumpers and free climbers know well. There is certainly a rigid routine to both preparing to and going through with hurling yourself off a cliff with only a pair of man-made wings sown into your bodysuit. Following this routine the first time is—I can only imagine—as much terrifying as exhilarating. You can only know, truly know, the routine works after you've tried it yourself and found it to be successful. What's interesting is that the more you embrace this same routine, the less your brain perceives the risk, even though the risk is technically the same as it was the first time.

The psychology behind this is simple: the more we repeat a risky action that rewards us, the less our brains translate the risk in a logical way. At some point, the emotion centers of our brains take over and we contemplate or perceive the risk emotionally. At first we consider the activity logically: "If I do this, I might die! Maybe I won't do this." But once we do it, the inner dialogue changes to: "I didn't die the first time so I probably won't die this time." After more repetition, that inner voice becomes more confident and we begin to anticipate the emotive reward from beginning to end. Eventually we say to ourselves, "If I do this, I will get this reward."

There's a mysterious element of routine that gives us the perception of control over our creative endeavors, even when the risk of failure still remains. It is this confidence that gives us the added fuel to go for it again, create more, risk more, venture into other frontiers. This is the reason why it is much easier for an elite adventure athlete like Mark Healey, who regularly surfs 30- to 60-foot waves, to learn other high-risk skills, like tagging hammerhead sharks for science.

In *Outside* magazine's March 2016 issue, Thayer Walker profiled the man big-wave surfing icon Laird Hamilton calls an "unrivaled" waterman, "unique even among us." At fourteen years old, Healey broke onto the surfing scene by riding 30-foot waves at Waimea Bay. He turned pro three years later and has been riding giant waves ever since. His ability to take risks and repeatedly experience the rare euphoria of flying down the face of a 60-foot wall of saltwater on a surfboard, which he did in 2014 at Jaws on Maui's North Shore, has allowed him to venture into other frontiers and create and innovate there. Those insane surfing scenes in the films *Chasing Mavericks* and *Point Break*, or the television series *Hawaii Five-O*? Mark Healey. He's become a go-to guy when it comes to risky water scenes, including work for a *National Geographic* television piece on great white sharks near Mexico's Guadalupe Island. He's also become an accomplished free diver, which is what he was doing when *Outside* magazine's Walker caught up with him.

He had joined a two-week scientific expedition to the waters around Mikomoto, Japan, where it was believed the hammerhead shark population had plummeted by about 90 percent due to overfishing. The scientists who Healey had joined were hoping to tag the hammerheads in order to track their patterns and find a creative solution for better conservation in the area. The guy doing the tagging, wearing only a wetsuit, fins, and a mask, was Healey. Because he can hold his breath for six minutes, the unrivaled waterman can dive deep below the surface, where the sharks swim, and place the tags on their dorsal fins, occasionally hanging for a brief ride when he can.

The work Mark Healey does is never without risk. He's fully aware that on any given day a giant wave or a giant fish could swallow him up. But what gives Healey such confidence in the face of danger is that he's been in the ocean his entire life. He grew up in Hawaii and learned to surf not long after he learned to walk. He's been diving, too, since he was a boy, as well as deep-sea fishing with his father. With each of these activities, Healey experienced time and again the importance of preparatory routine—passed down by his father—and the elation of reward side by side. Over time, the ocean has become far less a threat and far more a frontier ripe with mystery, possibility, and joy. Like life, the ocean always contains risk, especially if you dive into it. But it is only when you do so that you can experience such transcendent rewards.

"There are a lot of things working against people in this sport," he told Walker. "I take my preparation very seriously, but there are so many factors to longevity besides the odds of surviving something bad. . . . But it will never be safe. And the day that it is, I won't want to do it anymore."

Healey's approach to risk and reward might seem like yet another capricious idiosyncrasy, like Hemingway's bloodlust or Madame Curie's obsessiveness, that we assume separates great creators from the regular folks like us. But this is the cinematic view. Healey's

tolerance for danger is commensurate with his commitment to es-
tablishing a routine—as a child, in his case—that allowed him to
approach ventures with both skilled confidence and the emotional
freedom necessary to learn, adapt, and experience the full wonder
available to him. In this learned state he does not fall prey to the surf
industry's tendency to "bro you into bankruptcy" as he puts it. While
most professional surfers try to earn a better living by entering
more contests and seeking more sponsorships, Healey's penchant
for pushing boundaries has made him an innovative entrepreneur
whose latest company, Healey Water Ops, gives high-profile clients
the chance to experience the ocean like Healey does and swim with
sharks, spear giant tuna, and surf uncomfortably large waves. "I
would rather light myself on fire than go begging for pennies as a
grown man," Healey confessed to Walker. The reality, of course, is
that he doesn't have to because he's learned to keep the fire inside
him constantly stoked.

———

Let's not dance around the truth. There is no creative routine worth
embracing that is simultaneously light on risk and heavy on reward.
For that matter, there is nothing worth embracing in life of which
this is true. Lust is cheap. Love is costly. Cliché is easy. Originality is
difficult. But when it comes to how our creative ventures feel, that's
another matter. And this is where you must win the battle.

Our primary activity in life is creating. What we create determines the colors and contours of our lives. If we risk little, our

creations are predictable and life seems void of much value. If we risk much, our creations fill us with wonder and life is a gift.

The creative process is risk and reward at once all at once. Embracing a routine that ushers us into this lifestyle each day is a small price to pay, honestly. It may hurt at first, but the more you do it, the less risky and rote and unreasonable it will feel, even when your actual odds of failing haven't changed. Fighting this fight is one of the most worthwhile battles in your life.

Set about today to establish a routine, a rhythm, that allows you to maximize as much creative juice as possible every day, in every context you find yourself, with the tools you possess and those you are still learning.

Because everyone has idiosyncrasies, there is no more magic in certain activities than others. Just don't lie to yourself. Sleep in if it works best. Get up early if it's worse. Eat what fuels you and refrain from the other stuff. Don't get caught up in that immature business of rewarding yourself every hour of the day. Just because you spent an hour in a heady meeting doesn't mean you deserve a whiskey break. Do some really challenging work, stuff that stretches you— earn your rewards. This is the real effect of discipline: you embrace whatever routine sets you up for constant creative progress and the rewards come to you. And you can come to expect them. Like a lover who trusts his love to meet his needs, focus on what you have to give, not on what you will get.

I have been on tour for the last fourteen years. For eleven of those years, I have performed at least a hundred shows per year.

Different sights, cities, and people every other day for much of the year has made it critical to build a routine into my morning to connect my mind, body, and spirit every single day. I do not have the luxury of waiting until I'm home in the familiarity of my space and among my family members to follow a routine that fuels my creativity. My routine has to be fluid and effective wherever I am.

No matter what time zone I'm in, I wake up long before sunrise— usually at 4:00 A.M.—and open a devotional and read the short passage on a specific idea, thought, or contemplation from a spiritual mentor I admire. This takes me one to three minutes.

Then I relax into a brief period of meditation (five minutes). This is where I let go of my thoughts, desires, frustrations, or agendas. I empty the clutter bouncing around in my mind. I allow myself to enter a mental space of expansive calm without an agenda or a specific goal. I keep this period of meditation short so that I do not become overwhelmed with dutifully fulfilling a long obligation. This is about accessing and nurturing my oasis within before I ramp up to begin my very active day.

After the brief period of meditation, I write for fifteen to twenty-five minutes. This is when I connect with my wife, Tasha. We have been writing each other "good morning" e-mails every morning for fifteen years. There is no agenda or formula or expectation. It is completely stream of consciousness writing to connect us since we spend many mornings waking up in different parts of the world. Since I am usually awake first, I know that the first thing she will do to start her day is open the e-mail with my note. I often use my words to share insights from my morning devotional, to be vulnerable about my anxieties and joyful about my gratitude, and to share memorable details from a movie I watched or a conversation I had. This part of my routine helps both of us embrace empathy for one another and tap into a heightened state of emotional sensitivity. It also allows us to enter our days with refreshing honesty and hope. We have fifteen years of letters that archive the growth of our marriage, my art, our family, our business, my hopes, our faith, and our travels. If I am ever tempted to think I am not growing as a creator, I have only to read a few notes from past years to see where I was.

When I am done writing, I sip a double espresso—not to wake up, but rather because I associate the look, smell, and taste of a short, dark, crema-laden espresso with success. It fills my mind with anticipation and excitement for the day. I watch my hand bring the cup to my lips. I think about the espresso and smell the espresso. It might sound a bit dramatic but it's really just another deliberate act of connecting my mind and spirit to my body. I am sipping espresso and my mind is aware that I am sipping espresso. It reminds me that I am fully alive and fully present and have been given an incredible opportunity to create something beautiful that day. I then head to the gym for a rigorous workout. When I return from my workout, I fill the bathtub with hot water and soak in it for twenty to thirty minutes. During this time, I purposefully focus and visualize specific elements of my upcoming presentation, rehearsing them in my mind—the strokes of the brush, the music in concert with what I will say, the surprises I have for the audience. By the time it's 6:00 A.M., I'm ready for breakfast—but most important, I'm prepared for a creative explosion.

The importance lies not in what your routine involves but in whether it's effective. *Vogue* editor in chief Anna Wintour starts her day with a 5:45 A.M. tennis match. Disney CEO Robert Iger wakes at 4:30 A.M. to clear his head before heading off to another creative day; this head clearing involves exercise, reading the papers, surfing the Web, and watching a little TV. Oprah sits in stillness for twenty minutes twice a day. Padmasree Warrior, the chief technology and strategy officer of Cisco Systems, who oversees tens of thousands of employees, meditates daily and spends her Saturdays completely unplugged.

Know yourself and know what is important to you. Do what you have to do to innovate and elevate those priorities. Fight to establish and keep your creative routine. It is the one undercurrent that will amplify all else you do. It will push and pull you around at first, but once you get used to it, you won't feel the tugs. This is the promise of a routine that drives meaningful sparks in your life. Don't wait to be in the mood. "Being in the mood to write, like being in the mood to make love, is a luxury that isn't necessary in a long-term relationship," writes Julia Cameron. "Just as the first caress can lead to a change of heart, the first sentence, however tentative and awkward, can lead to a desire to go just a little further." Seek those first caresses. Discover them, embrace them and then you will come to expect them.

Allow your routine to become part of who you are, part of your lifestyle. When you experience its rewards, even only a few times, you will be ready to lean further in, or, as American philosopher C. S. Peirce puts it, you will transition from perception to recognition.

In other words, you will comprehend what constant creators have known for centuries.

In his sixteenth-century classic *The Prince,* Niccolò Machiavelli lamented that the people of his day seemed to think courage meant suffering. He was adamant this was wrong. He believed strength and courage were the ability to do bold things. A creativity-inducing routine gives you that right kind of strength.

In his hauntingly beautiful book *Crazy for the Storm,* author Norman Ollestad illustrates how his upbringing, both wonderfully idyllic and painfully regimented, prepared him as an eleven-year-old boy not only to survive a plane crash that took the life of his father, but also to chase the complex and yet extraordinary opportunities of his life.

Ollestad grew up in Topanga Beach, California, and, like Mark Healey, learned to surf while still a toddler. The jacket of the book shows him strapped to his dad's back as an eighteen-month-old while his dad rides the last whitewash of a wave into shore. The author's father was a successful attorney and a man who understood the unique interplay between routine and creative freedom. As a boy, Ollestad often bucked the routine, which included the regular chores of childhood as well as the necessities of surfing. There was a way to prepare your board and a way to rinse it off and the right clothing to wear and the right place to store your board when you were done. Ollestad enjoyed surfing—he grew up around the epic surf culture of Malibu in the 1970s—but his dad seemed to treat it like a religion, especially when it came to his insistence that Norman rise early to surf and ride waves much too big for him. Over time, the boy learned that there was more to it all than becoming a better surfer. His dad was teaching him how to live life and approach the inherent sacrifices and risks involved in chasing your potential.

Halfway through the book, Ollestad describes the moment when his father's routine began to make sense. He and his father were on a surfing adventure along the Mexican coast when they were forced to elude gun-wielding drug traffickers bent on robbing them. Their escape route led them to a native village bordering a beach that hosted perfect waves.

One early morning, against his wishes, Ollestad joined his father in the big surf that broke outside a dangerous coral reef. The boy was resentful at his dad—this man who was supposed to protect him knew full well how scared it made him. Reluctantly, Ollestad paddled out to the lineup only to watch his father, an experienced surfer, get pitched from a wave and onto the jagged reef, where he came up with blood pouring from a gash in his back.

The elder Ollestad shrugged off the wound and beckoned his son to join him in the risky break.

"I was numb. In a state of shock," writes the author. "Yet, in that moment, I would have rather died than succumb to my cowardice."

Ollestad noticed that smaller sets were breaking inside the bigger ones that had pummeled his dad. Though he "shook with adrenaline," he started paddling for them.

A 4-footer caught his eye. It still crossed over the reef, making it a dangerous proposition, but the younger Ollestad knew his father would prod him until he paddled into a wave. He pounced on the wave, standing up as the board pitched down the face. He fought nose-diving into the shallow water that hid the sharp coral below him, eventually stabilizing himself in the wave's trough. He then dug his board back up into the center of the wave as its lip began to curl. He crouched and leaned into the wall of water.

"The lip eclipsed the sun and the face of the wave turned dark blue," he explains.

> My brain protested. A wall of water is threatening to collapse onto you. Bail out.
>
> A voice, some kind of knowing force, told me—it opens up. It wraps around. You will fit inside. . . .
>
> Automatically my knees drew up to my chest and the board climbed into the pocket. My eyes closed as I entered the tube.
>
> The groan rumbled. I opened my eyes. An oval window framed the sand spit. The rock spires. The coconut palms. And the groan sucked away and the spinning cavern was silent. The ominous wall had bent and wrapped me in its peaceful womb. I was buried inside a thing that could maim or kill me, yet was cuddling me now—I was stretched between panic and bliss. Everything essential, everything formerly invisible, burst forth and pulsed through me.

After Ollestad reappeared from the tube, his father hollered out his approval and paddled to him. "You've been to a place that very few people in this world have ever gone," Mr. Ollestad said. "Someplace beyond all the bullshit."

As the two rode on their bellies into shore, Ollestad remembered looking around and thinking that the strange world suddenly made perfect sense. In recounting the epic moment while sitting around a fire with the Mexican villagers that evening, the senior Ollestad leaned to his son and told him what a pretty teenage local had said of the experience of riding in a tube.

"She said it was a doorway to heaven."

The boy agreed, then remembered the razor-sharp reef.

"But you could get crushed and shredded. Maybe even die."

"That's life, Ollestad," his dad calmly replied.

Ollestad stared at the flames rising from the fire and thought: "Beautiful things were sometimes mixed up with treacherous things, they could even happen at the same time, or one could lead to the other."

Yes, Mr. Ollestad, that's life . . . and the pursuit of creativity that makes us come alive.

5

DEFAMILIARIZE THE ORDINARY

Genius is only a superior power of seeing.

—**John Ruskin**

HAVE YOU HEARD THE STORY OF SUPERSTAR QUARTER-back Tom Brady giving back his Super Bowl rings? Or the story about Apple asking to be removed from the top spot on Interbrand's list of the 100 most valuable brands in the world? What about the story of the latest winner of the Nobel Prize in science turning down the award?

No, you haven't. Because the stories never happened. You might be tempted to think such stories never happen. But at least one creative genius turned down warranted recognition in the name of greater creativity.

The man's name is Antoine Westermann, a French-born chef

who now presides over five highly touted restaurants—three in his hometown of Paris and two in New York City. Westermann wanted to be a great chef from the age of eight, after watching his parents serve the family and their many guests delicious meals. It was his parents, however, who discouraged him from the challenging life of a chef. He didn't listen. At fourteen, Westermann took a job as an apprentice cook at a railway station café in Strasbourg, France. A few years later, he moved to Paris to work in the great kitchens there, later seeking formal training at a culinary institute.

By the time he was twenty-three, Westermann was a formidable chef who'd proven his parents wrong. He returned home to Alsace, where his proud father took out a mortgage on their family home and lent it to him to start his first restaurant, Le Buerehiesel. Within six years, Westermann had not only earned a reputation as one of the best chefs in the country, he'd also won his first Michelin star.

Nine years later, in 1983, Westermann was awarded his second Michelin star for his now world-acclaimed restaurant.

Then, in 1994, at the age of forty-eight, Westermann did it—he won his third Michelin star, the absolute peak of culinary recognition, akin to a physicist winning a Nobel Prize, a sprinter winning an Olympic gold medal, or a golfer winning the Masters.

Westermann capitalized on the recognition by opening multiple restaurants in France, one in Portugal, and another in the United States over the decade that followed. His name was synonymous with greatness and his restaurants were never empty.

Then, at the height of his career, he did something no one

expected. Chef Westermann contacted the Michelin judges and asked for his three stars to be removed.

When Michelin asked the reason for his absurd request, he told them "so his creativity would no longer be confined by the rules and regulations of the guide." In essence, he was saying to the judges who establish the standards for the Michelin guidebook that perhaps he would define his own standards. His creativity would no longer live under a ceiling; he would not strive merely for the ordinary pinnacle of culinary mastery. The judges had little choice but to accept his request and his name and restaurant were removed from the guide.

Westermann began to travel as a consultant to chefs around the world. It was during his travels that he was introduced to a new generation of American farmers, particularly in the northeastern part of the country. Possibilities exploded as Westermann observed and learned their ways. In the years that followed, he explored new culinary tendencies. He opened two restaurants in Paris that he calls sandwich bars, then another in Portugal that serves only appetizers. His latest creation is a restaurant in New York City called Le Coq Rico, which opened in 2016. It pays homage to his all-time favorite dish: poultry.

Why would a chef at the height of the culinary world trade three Michelin stars for a chicken restaurant? He explains it this way: "I realized that the cuisine I create . . . would not be accessible to most people who dine out—it's too expensive. I had been cooking that way for all of my professional life and there was a point at which I decided I wanted to offer something else, for myself and for others."

Instead of striving to meet his industry's standard of excellence as long as possible, he decided to recreate the standard. And a new level of originality (and tastiness) was born.

To grind your sparks and spark your grind . . .
DEFAMILIARIZE THE ORDINARY

At times a small shift can be a catalyst for great results. At other times, a full-scale change is required to get us out of a rut and show us a better, more efficient, more creative path. Either way, we have a choice in the matter. We can wait for that catalyst to come to us and then struggle to spark a solution on the fly—essentially placing our bet on agility. Or we can originate the catalyst ourselves and develop an instinct that keeps creative sparks close at hand.

While nearly everyone has experienced a "spark" of creativity, most struggle to call it up at will. Even fewer live in a constant state of creativity. But those who do are potent, vibrant people in any environment. And you can be one.

Despite all the planning and forecasting involved in running your life, constant creativity hinges on your ability to regularly enter unfamiliar space and cultivate your creative instinct.

"Those who profess to favor freedom," wrote Frederick Douglass, "and yet depreciate agitation, are men who want rain without thunder and lightning." Seeds never germinate without a dormant season called winter. Fields never turn green without regular storms; but they also never grow without a break in the clouds allowing sunlight to shine through. The natural world is a constant reminder that progress never occurs without some change to the familiar.

The key is to ignite that lack of familiarity yourself. Don't avoid it. And don't wait for it to come.

———

We take advantage of what we know.

We abuse it, really.

Then its returns diminish over time.

And we either stop and wonder what the hell happened to us. Or we don't wonder at all. We just keep operating on less and less new knowledge, less and less cognitive fuel. Less and less awareness. We don't even know the extent of it. Or its significance. But deep down we feel it.

Life slowly fades to a less vibrant scene. It becomes more predictable, sadly predictable and same-same. Eventually it's monochrome.

Monochrome is popular these days. Look at all the photo filters on your phone and Instagram-like apps. Through those lenses life takes on a mysterious, ethereal aesthetic. At a glance, everyday reality looks more artful—in fact, more artful than it really is. But we often ignore this fact because we don't know how else to make life more beautiful other than through an alien lens.

The key is to own that alien lens by learning to see your own life in an unfamiliar way, like a stranger meeting you for the first time. Constant creators do this intuitively. The good news is, it's a learned intuition.

Sparks arise when you discover nuances you hadn't seen before and connections you'd never made. That takes a lens that constantly searches for the unfamiliar and zooms in to have a better look—both within yourself and in the environment around you. "Mystery is at the heart of creativity," writes Julia Cameron. "That, and surprise."

A short path to igniting sparks is to either see things differently or see different things. The fact is that original breakthroughs rarely occur in locations with which we are familiar. This includes the space in our own minds where we carry our preconceived notions about the people and places around us and where current knowledge resides. So the trick is to remove yourself from your familiar places, or else discover what is unfamiliar where you already are. Both are productive options. Dr. Paul Billings chose the latter.

Dr. Billings spent the first decade of his career working in the emergency room at Athens Regional Hospital in the bustling college town of Athens, Georgia. There, he proved to be a talented and compassionate physician, a gift to his emergency room patients, and an inspiration to his coworkers. He didn't set out just to know names and medical histories. He wanted to know the hearts of his patients. And so he did, especially those he saw often: the young woman fighting a drug addiction so she could give her two kids a better life; the middle-aged Hispanic man who struggled to find steady work but wanted desperately to make a good life for himself and his wife; the homeless man in his sixties who hoped aloud that his children would one day forgive him.

Before long it became clear that Dr. Billings was an outlier in a segment of the medical profession that rarely finds time to be anything but clinical. No matter what sent you to the hospital in Athens, Georgia, Dr. Billings was who you hoped to see when you arrived. That sort of reputation was eventually impossible to ignore, and by his midthirties, he was promoted to the head of the ER.

The story could end there and we could mine a nice lesson from how a doctor used an uncommon level of compassion to re-create a typically precise and steely environment. But that's not where Dr. Billings's story ends.

Doctors in the ER often get a daily glimpse into the socioeconomic struggles of their cities: drugs, poverty, prostitution, abuse, to name only a few. Some doctors ignore the deeper problems and focus on what they know, the work they were trained to do—one suture, one surgery, one diagnosis at a time. Other doctors lament over what they see to their colleagues and spouses, but feel helpless to make any real difference. It's just not their line of work. So they, too, focus on doing the work they've been trained to do.

Dr. Billings doesn't think this way. When he sees a problem, he seeks a solution—even if it's beyond what he has been trained to do. When he realized how many of his repeat patients were not drug addicts or alcoholics but rather good people trying to make ends meet who simply couldn't afford health insurance, a spark ignited.

He knew these patients were not trying to be a drain on the system; they were usually embarrassed when their visit to the ER ended up being a minor issue. But what else could they do? They couldn't afford to see a doctor for checkups or a diagnosis. They couldn't visit a specialist to receive prescriptions for medicine that would heal them much quicker. So they often did nothing, hoping a sickness or injury or strange feeling would just pass. When it didn't, they did what most of us would do—they sought out the only doctor they could afford—the ER doctor who by law would treat them even if they had no money.

Knowing all this—and knowing the hearts of many of these patients, who were trying to do well in life—Dr. Billings asked himself: *Was there any way to dignify these well-meaning patients with regular, preventative care so they didn't have to use the ER like a family doctor?*

As he thought about this question, it became clearer and clearer that the answer was no, at least not in the current environment in which he worked. But when he considered another environment unfamiliar to him at the time—private practice—the answer leaned toward yes.

It would take nearly two years, several volunteers, and the financial commitment of many local business owners and, yes, fellow physicians who caught the doctor's vision, but approximately fourteen years after taking the Hippocratic oath, Dr. Billings put in his notice at Athens Regional Hospital and took a 40 percent pay cut to assume the role of director and head physician of his brainchild, the Mercy Health Center, a one-of-a-kind health services provider where patients are treated with preventative measures and for health issues as they arise—just as they would be in a family doctor's office. And they are asked only to pay what they can.

In a familiar environment, Dr. Billings sought the unfamiliar and discovered the spark of a creation that is changing the lives of thousands of good people in a typically marginalized population.

Have you taken time to discover what is unfamiliar about your life, your career, or your primary roles that might provide a spark for growth and progress? Do you know where the hidden sparks lie in your environment?

You probably know at least some, even if you've been prone to ignoring them—enough to start, for sure. The first step is to begin digging into these unfamiliar areas. Stretch to see them. Contemplate them. Mull them over and over. And never cease.

Could it be that what you don't know does hurt you? It's true if you desire constant creativity. The path of your current knowledge, your current know-how, your current understanding is never enough if you want to remain on the creative frontiers. You must peer down the path of the unknown and unfamiliar if you want to continue generating sparks. If you don't know where to begin, start, as Friar Richard Rohr said, by saying "I don't know anything."

It's truer than asserting we know everything. And when we start with no knowledge, suddenly discovery is our primary resource. It is far easier to reach this conclusion about yourself—that your knowledge is limited or truly nil—when you begin to comprehend the vastness of opportunities and miracles around you every day.

Two centuries ago, the poet William Blake offered us an incredible possibility:

To see a World in a Grain of Sand
And a Heaven in a Wild Flower,
Hold Infinity in the palm of your hand
and Eternity in an hour

"Yeah, that would be nice," confesses Adam Frank in a commentary on NPR. "Unfortunately, most of us don't know how. . . . Tumbling through the chaos of our day-to-days, we wonder if Blake's vision . . . is nothing more than a poet's fancy. Can we really see the Universe in a grain of sand[?] . . . The answer, I believe, is 'yes,'" Frank admits. "How do I know this? Because I am a scientist dammit and I know that . . . we walk past a thousand natural miracles everyday, from the sun climbing in the sky to the arc of birds seen out our windows. Those miracles are there waiting for us to see them, to notice them and, most importantly, to find our delight in theirs."

The trick, says Frank, is in the noticing.

If you've had the pleasure of watching the documentary *Jiro Dreams of Sushi*, you witnessed an artist in action who routinely extracts the extraordinary from the seemingly mundane, from an element of our lives we easily overlook: food. Jiro is a great noticer of the smallest sparks in his work—and this is a primary trait that makes him an astonishing creator.

Jiro Ono is an eighty-five-year-old sushi chef who is widely considered the best in the world. He runs Sukiyabashi Jiro, a modest restaurant that thousands pass every day without a glance. The film is a study of Jiro's uncanny ability to notice the details that differentiate an ordinary piece of sushi from an extraordinary one—details that set him apart from thousands of sushi chefs the world over.

A unique characteristic of the film is that we learn about Jiro's ways from those who are learning from him. He is a man of few words, and consistent action, which is what it no doubt takes to be as attentive to the details as he is. An apprentice of Jiro's says it best:

"There is so much you can't learn from words." This is Jiro's way. We learn from his son, whom he is training to take over some day, that Jiro believes "each ingredient has an ideal moment of deliciousness." Notice it's not each piece of sushi—it's each ingredient, even when a piece of sushi has, in some cases, only three or four ingredients. This is why Jiro and his son spend countless hours inspecting and testing each fish at the fish market before they buy one. "Mastering the timing of sushi is difficult," Jiro's son explains. "It takes . . . experience to develop your intuition."

This is an important point. To develop your intuition, you must spend more than one day each year ruminating on the details of your life. You have to spend more than one day a month. More than one day a week. To develop your creative intuition—your instinct to spot sparks in the seemingly mundane details of your existence— you must contemplate and meditate on your life, your career, your relationships, your roles . . . yourself, daily.

This doesn't mean you have to hole up in a yoga studio or monastery for an hour every morning. For constant creators, the instinct is cultivated and made habitual in small moments throughout the day. Instead of assuming anything, they learn to ponder a moment more. The sum of this is what Steven Pressfield calls fighting the resistance. "Most of us," he writes in *The War of Art,* "have two lives. The life we live, and the unlived life within us. Between the two stands resistance. . . . Its target is the epicenter of our being: our genius, our soul, the unique and priceless gift we were put on earth to give and that no one else has but us. Resistance . . . is the dragon that guards the gold."

Resist living in the shallows of your environment. Resist water-skiing over the surface and living only for the sum of the experience. Consider the ingredients that make the experience what it is—the people, the words, the emotions, the meaning, the combinations and collisions. Sparks live there, at times just a moment beyond the second most reach the common conclusion. Jiro does this masterfully in his work as a chef. Few see it as he does. But because he takes the time to see it, anyone can taste the mastery in his creations.

When Jiro's restaurant received a perfect three Michelin stars, which means it's worth traveling to that country just to eat there, those who'd never tried his sushi were astonished. There are only ten seats in his restaurant. It's located in a Tokyo subway station. Yet sushi lovers and foodies the world over still make reservations months in advance and gladly—giddily—make the trek every year, while thousands of others continue to rush by on their way to work or lunch or errands, without ever realizing they've passed greatness.

In a piece for online magazine Quartz, Carolyn Gregoire and Scott Barry Kaufman detail one of history's most fascinating creativity studies, conducted by psychologist Frank X. Barron in the 1960s. Barron set out to understand the genesis of great creativity—the elusive spark. To do so, he invited his generation's most renowned writers, architects, scientists, entrepreneurs, and mathematicians to live in a former frat house on the University of California, Berkeley campus. The participants spent time socializing and were evaluated on this and other things. Assessments of their lives, work, and per-

K
**********2896

The spark and the grind : ignite
anf
33305238665107

Expires 06/03/18
Sun

sonalities were conducted, and tests geared to uncovering signs of mental illness and creative thought were given. Barron's overarching discovery was contrary to convention at the time, which assumed great creators relied heavily on above-average intelligence. This, as it turned out, played a minor role.

"Instead," write Gregoire and Kaufman, "the study showed that creativity is informed by a whole host of . . . characteristics." The common traits of every creative person in Baron's study? "An openness to one's inner life; a preference for complexity and ambiguity; an unusually high tolerance for disorder and disarray; the ability to extract order from chaos; independence; unconventionality; and a willingness to take risks."

In other words, great creators are quite a contradiction. Compelled by these complex results, Gregoire and Kaufman point out that Frank X. Barron conducted a subsequent study on creative writers with Donald MacKinnon, a psychology professor who had helped select Secret Service agents in World War II. They found that the average writer scored high on all measures of psychopathology, but equally high on all measures of psychological health.

Baron and MacKinnon concluded that the reason for this contradiction was that constant creators were regularly introspective, which led to a steady self-awareness and an ability to "engage with the full spectrum of life." In other words, say Gregoire and Kaufman, "in both their creative processes and their brain processes, they bring seemingly contradictory elements together in unusual and unexpected ways."

While an unexpected mash-up happens occasionally in our

lives—for example, you realize that your being a former Division 1 athlete has already primed you to succeed as a salesperson—most unexpected combinations in our lives don't simply come to us. We have to search for them in the recesses of our experience and let our brains do what they do and make associations that we'd never considered before. Sure, some of are more naturally inclined to do this. Their brains are a little wilder, to use Natalie Goldberg's phrase, than the average person. But this is no excuse for the rest of us.

Remember, every one of us has a neurological network that simultaneously seeks efficiency and novelty. By introducing ourselves to the unfamiliar, we open up our network to novel possibilities for efficiency. This is called innovation.

In order to introduce unfamiliarity into my life on a regular basis, I attempt to learn something new at least once a year, something I have no legitimate experience with. Two years ago, I decided I'd learn to play poker like a pro. Like many, I'd played a hand or two with friends. But outside of my hatred of losing, I'd never had any compelling interest in becoming a legitimate poker player. The world of real poker, with real stakes, and professionals all around the table, was very unfamiliar to me.

To make sure I was fully engaged in the effort, I entered myself in the World Series of Poker main event in Las Vegas. All the big names would be there. And me, a nobody. I had four months to prepare. My goal was to deconstruct poker down to its most simplistic form and then reconstruct it so that I could play freely, efficiently, and without emotion.

I asked the Duchess of Poker, Annie Duke, who has raked in

over $4 million in winnings, to coach and mentor me. Simultaneously, I read half a dozen books on tournament strategy. I memorized the mathematical probability charts. I studied game theory and the human psychology of revealing and discovering tells. Then I played ten thousand flops to condition myself to the rigor of the two 12-hour days at the tournament.

I entered the tournament as prepared as I could be and played well for nearly twelve hours on the first day. I had a very nice stack of chips that would give me momentum going into day two of the tournament. The day was winding down, with a couple of minutes left, and blinds were up to two hundred to four hundred dollars and antes fifty dollars. Play was very loose, with players pushing rubbish cards in an effort to steal blinds in a last-ditch effort to build their stacks. It was at this point that I was dealt pocket kings. I had just folded twice on an ace-king hand so I had set this up beautifully. The other players wouldn't suspect the hand I held. I did not want to see a flop and risk an ace falling on the board, so I raised aggressively against a notorious stealer in the poker world and he reraised as he had done several times before, with nothing to protect his blinds. I shoved all my chips forward, given every previous read I had on this cat. And I ran smack into his pair of pocket aces. The crowd and the other players at the table went wild when they saw us throw down a pair of kings and a pair of aces. It happens. Not often. But it happens. And I was on the losing end big time.

I was disappointed—I had considerable leverage for day two. But the disappointment passed quickly and I saw the day as one of the most exhilarating experiences of my life. While the tournament had sparked some interesting thoughts in me—about discipline, probability, risk, to name the main topics—the real sparks from this unfamiliar venture came when I debriefed with Annie.

I told her that I felt I played "twelve hours of nearly flawless poker" until the moment I got taken out by the pair of aces. She immediately corrected me. In thirty years of professional poker, she said, she had never played fifteen minutes of flawless poker. There are just too many variables in every hand. The game contains too much uncertainty. But, she pointed out, this is not what derails good players who never become great. What really happens is that they believe they reach a point where they know enough, where the game is just a matter of probability or of perfecting bluffing or stealing blinds. These players aren't innovative enough to understand that poker requires a great deal of creativity and some profoundly good timing. The greatest players know this and they have a way of learning anew each hand.

While the greats take into each hand what they know about the other players—who's safe and who's aggressive—and what they know about the cards on the table, they don't ever lean too much into this knowledge. They also lean into the uncertainty and make a concerted effort to learn there in a way they hadn't before so they can play in a way nobody expects. There is no such thing, she said, as flawless poker, just the constant pursuit of it, which firmly plants you in the land of uncertainty. The irony, however, is that it's the player who is able to inject uncertainty into her opponents who ultimately has the edge.

It is very easy to beat players who always play the same way—just as it is easy to out-innovate a company that continues to churn out the same product or service. If a player is conservative, I will fold when they decide to enter the pot. If a player is liberal, I will play tight and play only strong cards. When your opponent becomes predictable you can easily decide whether to be aggressive or passive and by doing so avoid big mistakes. But being able to become unpredictable yourself is what ultimately elevates your game to another level. This is why creativity is the true ace in your hand.

In my first foray into professional poker, I proved huge strides in my ability to read the predictability of other players. But when I came up against another player—a real pro—who was gifted at reading me, I fell victim to my own predictability. I didn't defamiliarize my own game enough and when the pro could see I was confident enough to go all in, he knew he could take me out completely with his aces.

"In battle," wrote Sun Tzu in *The Art of War*, "there are not more than two methods of attack—direct and the indirect; yet these two in combination give rise to an endless series of maneuvers."

The goal of all great creations is to remove complexity and move toward simplicity. To do this, though, you have to enter into the complexity, the uncertainty, the unfamiliar. No two days are the same, just as no two poker hands are the same. Success in the past never guarantees success in the future. To ignite fresh sparks, you must decide to play your hand each day as uniquely as possible, removing the assumptions of historical precedent. Your brain has what you know from past experience locked in. It's in the bank, so to speak. But the sparks that come from that reservoir are ever diminishing unless you add fresh data to it every day—unless you mix the familiar with the unfamiliar.

It is the newly stoked fires that ignite you and give your life new meaning. New begets new. Old begets old. You must go after what is new, which is never familiar at first.

A lack of creativity is fundamentally a lack of curiosity. It is a lack of desire and a latent drive to seek new answers. That drive is in you. But with it in neutral or turned off entirely, you easily cling to a binary view of the world. Things are black or white. Good or bad. Part of your tribe or alien to it.

On the other hand, living curiously is fully embracing the moment and searching for connections in the in-between. Practice by letting this moment seize you now. Take a breath and live fully present in it. Let everything that's happening to you happen. Don't edit. Feel the clarity and confusion. The gain and loss. The creative journey is uncertain and may hurt you. But clinging to the same certainties will kill you. Stay open to whatever comes with the uncertainty. Breathe it in. Digest it. Fold it into your perspective and understanding. Let everything begin to teach you.

We like the way things are—especially when they've been that way for a long time. If it ain't broke, don't fix it, right? There's nothing wrong with that statement, generally speaking. When you get something right, there's no reason not to run with it. And stick with it. No need to reinvent the wheel, as they say.

Unless . . . there's something better.

Here's the truth constant creators cling to: there is always something better, in this life, anyhow.

A few look for it. Most try to live without it. Eventually we all comply with the better way and enjoy the benefits. Only a few actually profit from it.

The trouble is that we are not daring people in familiar situations. When nothing is broken or worrisome or unclear, we tend not to ask questions, we dial down our curiosity. When things are fine, we leave well enough alone. We find our groove and stay in it until it's five feet eleven inches deep. Then we realize it's killing us.

That sums up the most common path to mediocrity.

No one would mind if breakthroughs were born out of comfort. Unfortunately, they aren't. They are captured in the midst of uncertainty and complexity.

"Naturally," wrote Oswald Chambers, "we are inclined to be so mathematical and calculating that we look upon uncertainty as a bad thing. . . . Certainty is the mark of the common-sense life; gracious uncertainty is the mark of the spiritual life."

Either we enter uncertainty willingly, or we wait until it comes to us. If we wait, it usually comes when we are not prepared.

The irony is that it's far safer to enter the chaos of our own volition than to wait for it to arrive. Because chaos doesn't knock. It doesn't even enter through the front door. It smashes through the back window and takes us by surprise. Sometimes we don't recover.

This is a lesson being learned in the car service industry right now. For decades, cabs and limos served the masses. One is the low-cost provider. The other the high-cost provider. Neither have changed in decades. Both were in their grooves, comfortable, albeit not immune to the fluctuations of the economy. Generally speaking, both cabs and limos had a good thing going. No need to reinvent the wheel(s), right?

Then along came the uncertainty called Uber. And its tagline: "Everyone's private driver."

Uber simultaneously attacked both the low-end and high-end providers in the industry by upending long-held conventions. A few innovators placed a bet that we would pay a slight premium over cab fare—or get a large discount on limo fare—for an on-call car service we could summon with our smartphones. One that was predictably excellent. One that removed the time-consuming transaction and tip from the process. One that utilized the most modern technology. One that literally put the controls in consumers' hands and turned the process of procuring urban transportation into a convenient, viral experience.

Until a couple of years ago, I used cabs. On rare occasions, I scheduled a town car. Then a friend opened an iPhone app and touched a button while we finished espressos. Ten minutes later a shiny black Tahoe appeared at the curb in front of the San Diego café where we sat. As I watched his car drive off, I downloaded the Uber app. I've never gone back to the old way.

Cabs and limos are now fighting for their lives. If they survive, they won't be the same iterations of the past several decades. In fact, as recently as the spring of 2016, yellow cabs are now promoting a new app that effectively allows riders to hail and pay for a cab through the app, much like the Uber experience.

There's not just an entrepreneurial lesson here. Our lives are just as susceptible to the cab-and-limo mentality. Familiarity is a common sign of mediocrity. And mediocrity never made a single one of us happy or successful. Unexpected chaos in this context only makes life worse—a tangled web of confusion, disillusion, frustration, and often surrender.

Fortunately, there is an Uber in all of us. Multiple ones, actually. They're those little itches inside—some call them thorns—that won't go away. They nag us to keep exploring beyond what we know, what we assume, what we accept, and into that uncertain frontier called possibility. They beckon us to do it willingly, proactively. Listen to them (and me, if you don't mind). Don't hesitate. Don't analyze. Just get yourself beyond what you haven't changed for years or decades. Despite the discomfort. Regardless of the fear. That's where your creative frontier begins.

Breakthrough creations are born in the recesses, shadows, and depths to which we don't typically travel. Go there, and in going there you will bring them out into the light, even if only to remind yourself that your existence has far more to offer than what you know and plainly see. Remember that you have to be a traveler, not a tourist. Set out to discover novelty and insight in what is unfamiliar— which is where it is usually found. Don't set out merely to find what you already know is there.

There's something to be said for tradition, but if you're aiming to be more creative more often, you're going to find it increasingly difficult to discover newness and vitality on your tenth trip to Disneyland.

Familiarity numbs the senses. You've heard of having "new eyes"? This is what it means when you see something right in front of you, or inside you, as if for the first time. And this can happen with all your senses.

Sometimes all that is needed is a small perspective change. This is the reason I don't ever sell my paintings. Instead, I either donate them to fund-raisers or I give them away through Art Drops, a Facebook and Twitter treasure hunt in which I hide paintings in random locations in the cities where I am speaking, then tweet a clue about the location. The only price to play the game is the willingness to enter into an unfamiliar territory, into mystery. The obvious reward is the painting, if you find it. But even if you don't win the painting, there is a benefit in getting outside your typical workday to explore. Art Drops are a metaphor for how I'd like you to approach life: as an inspector, not an expecter. It's also a tangible example of how I want to remain as a creator and entrepreneur.

The world is full of artists who sell their paintings on the retail market or through auction houses, but I want to push those boundaries. I don't sell art as a commodity. Conventional wisdom encourages a marketplace of supply and demand. By disallowing supply, I've chosen instead to drive value that has no comparable price tag. The paintings cannot be bought in the traditional way. But they must still be sought out.

The self-proclaimed Wizard of Ads Roy Williams once compared the genesis of creativity to the earthquakes that cause subterranean plates to rise and form plateaus. "Pressure, pressure, pressure unspeakable then BANG the world breaks open and a plateau pops up from solid rock." He references the Balcones escarpment near his home outside Austin, Texas, which, despite its formation some 12 million years ago, still features "massive artesian springs gushing tens of millions of gallons per day."

It's a perfect metaphor, Williams says, for the release of creativity.

We get dried up when we rely on the familiar, the known, the comfortable in our lives. Eventually, something in us starts to stir. If we investigate this stirring, if we're daring enough to poke and prod it, we break open to new possibilities sooner and the artesian springs within us come gushing out to meet them.

If we don't—if we ignore the stirring—it might rumble harmlessly for a while as life grows drier and drier. Until . . . until a circumstance forces that rumbling to the surface. This usually happens when something unexpected occurs in your life and you are shoved out of your comfort zone before you know what's happening.

Williams once mentioned to his longtime friend, a psychologist named Richard D. Grant, that he always had his best ideas on the plane rides home after speaking engagements. "Well of course," his friend replied. "Working to connect to an audience is an extraverted [sic] feeling, your least preferred function." When Dr. Grant saw Williams was confused, he explained, "Psychologists have known for years that a person's least preferred function is the trap door to the unconscious mind."

Essentially, the psychologist friend was telling Williams that he was most creative when his familiar M.O. was no longer enough, forcing him to unearth the creative wellspring inside him and operate in a new way. "We almost never go there," concludes Williams. "But when we do—even if we stay there only briefly . . . [m]illions of gallons of creativity come sparkling into the sunlight through the crack created by that earthquake."

You can wait for the earthquake to come or you can get it started yourself. Constant creators do this regularly. Williams offers the story of an aspiring musician named Herb as a great example of what can happen when you do.

In 1955, Herb was a trumpet player in the marching band at USC. After college, he worked his craft, trying his best to improve and chase down some success. What musician doesn't want to play music for a living? Seven years later, Herb was grinding in his garage, attempting to track a jazz trumpet song called "Twinkle Star," when he decided he needed a break. The sparks weren't flying. He drove two hours to the San Diego–Mexico border and into Tijuana to watch the bullfights.

As he observed the pomp and circumstance, he breathed in the carefree sounds of the trumpet section in the stands as it announced each new event. There was something affecting and profound about those untroubled trumpets in that multicolored, emotionally ambiguous setting on a breezy, warm Tijuana afternoon. The foreign encounter moved him in an unexpected way, stuck with him, and although he couldn't put his finger on why, he knew he'd found the spark of something that could ignite his grind back home.

Herb jotted some mental notes and then returned to his garage, where he immediately renamed the song he had been working on, "Twinkle Star," to "The Lonely Bull," and infused it with the capricious notes of the Tijuana arena. Then he recorded it and sent it to some radio stations.

The song quickly became a Top 10 hit and won Herb some cash and a budding popularity, so he hired a few musicians and created an album of this same unique, Latin-infused jazz. Their music took off. Really took off.

In 1966, four years after Herb paid that visit to Tijuana, his band sold more records than the Beatles. Keep in mind, this is when the Beatles were, according to John Lennon, "more popular than Jesus." Apparently, not more than Herb's band, though, whose sales continued to rise.

When it was all said and done, their works garnered:

Five number 1 hits.
Fifteen gold albums.
Fourteen platinum albums.
Eight Grammy Awards.
Sales of seventy-two million albums.

You think you'd know all about them. But I'm guessing you don't.

The band called themselves Herb Alpert and the Tijuana Brass. To this day, they are the only band in history to have four albums in the Top 10 simultaneously.

By the way, Herb and bandmate Jerry Moss decided to start their own record label in 1969. They named it after the first letters in their last names: A&M Records. Twenty years later, Herb and Jerry sold A&M to PolyGram for $500 million.

It all happened from a trip beyond the ordinary confines of one young man's familiar environment. There, a new world he could never have imagined opened up to him . . . and everybody who listened to his creations.

No creator is immune to creative slumps. I certainly am not. I slide into creative funks often brought on by too much familiarity in my daily schedule. In fact, I like to think of creative funks as a reminder to change things up in a more radical way, to embrace a new kind of unfamiliarity. While my militaristic discipline keeps me honest and ensures I am grinding efficiently, I am still susceptible to recurring problems or staleness in my career or marriage or parenthood when I fail to regularly usher foreignness into my schedule. There are two ways I approach this: short-term shocks to my system and long-term solutions. The short-term shocks are for immediate use, in the moment, when I'm hitting a wall and need a jolt to wake me up. The long-term solutions are constantly evolving methods I use to keep me feeling unfamiliar (and even uncomfortable) every day.

Let me offer a caveat here before I go into the specifics of my strategies. Getting out of creative slumps is rarely as simple as changing your scenery or Pandora stations (which I realize can be seen as miniventures into the unfamiliar). While every now and then a new view or vibe can improve your mood and get you through a rut, such strategies aren't reliable for uncovering your creative embers on a regular basis. Their success rate is unpredictable at best, unlikely at worst. I could go into more low-hanging strategies like these but I don't want you to stay in slumps for longer than you have to. That's why I'm going to cut to the chase: getting out of creative slumps requires some physical effort and inconvenience. Sometimes that means getting off your butt or out of your head for a time.

Slumps happen when our minds are not introduced to enough new stimuli, so that they become too efficient for our creative good. We therefore need to shake them up, jolt ourselves out of cerebral mode, become irrational and inefficient for a time, so our minds are forced out of their comfort zone and into the land of abstraction, heightened senses, and emotion.

This is why the two most effective short-term ways to shock me out of a creative funk fall into the category some like to call "biohacking." I've found that when I change my physiology radically in a moment, it immediately changes my blood flow and limbic system (responsible for emotions and behavior) and therefore my mind-set. There are two ways I do this. The first is a polar plunge, or what is technically called cold thermogenesis or, more recently, cryotherapy. Subjecting myself to a shockingly cold ice bath, like the Pacific Ocean in winter or a cold shower, or a cryotherapy box at my local gym, immediately startles my mind out of any sort of slumber it might be in, creative ones included. When I'm in the middle of a day in my studio, working on a new painting or searching for a new way to engage my audiences, and I can feel my wheels just spinning, I stop what I'm doing and get in some icy cold water. The shock to my physical system sends a charge into my limbic system that always alters my mental state and helps me think and feel better.

The other short-term biohacking strategy to use is what your personal trainer might call heart-rate variability. I like to call it ballistic exercise instead, because it sounds more properly extreme. Fortunately, I am young and healthy enough so that this can be done without physical repercussions. If I find myself in a creative funk and need to break out of it right away, I will leave my studio or my hotel room for no more than five or ten minutes and run wind sprints in the parking lot, or in the stairwell, or find a hill and head up as fast as I possibly can. You don't have to do ballistic exercise long for it to begin releasing stress and pulsing a greater flow of blood through your body.

Ninety-nine percent of my job happens in the dark. Off the stage and out of the bright lights. I have found that if I do not intentionally shock my physiology, I can easily get too comfortable for my creative good. Calmer changes like naps, snack breaks, or walks in the woods don't change my mental or physical state enough to release creative energy for radical new ideas. I want to ignite shocking ideas. So I shock my system when I need to break from a creative slump.

I will admit, however, that I'm not always in a physical location or state where a polar plunge or wind sprints are possible. On a plane, for example, where I tend to spend a lot of time (that's a pretty narrow aisle). Or when sick or injured and temporarily experiencing some physical limitation. Likewise, if my options sound a little too public for you to do—or not practical because of where you work— then get a jump rope or just crank the music and dance like you mean it. But over the years I've also sought out more regular, long-term strategies that keep unfamiliarity flowing into my days.

One of my favorite strategies is fasting for a twenty-four-hour period once a month. I adopted this practice a couple of years ago and I can report that it has increased my creative output dramatically. Yes, fasting is also done for spiritual reasons. However, my particular practice is specifically to sacrifice comfort for creativity.

It can be argued that it is a precarious strategy to allow my blood sugar to dip and become more susceptible to fatigue. But when my fasting is scheduled, I make adjustments in my diet in the days leading up to the fast to ensure it's as successful as possible. As a result, my ability to delay gratification opens my mind to more ideas, fewer expectations, more experiences. It especially teaches me to remain patient and trust the process when my grind isn't igniting ideas and progress as I feel it should be. Believe me, if you can get past your irritability, your body, mind, and spirit become more connected. This is science, not my opinion. By fasting, especially for twenty-four hours, you are essentially placing your body into crisis mode, which causes it to feel, think, and act with greater clarity. Yes, at first you will feel and think largely about food. But if you make this a regular practice, you can train yourself to ignore the thoughts of In-N-Out Burger and Starbucks and focus your clarity on the full scope of creative opportunities before you. Of course, this kind of thing isn't for everyone. I'm not a doctor or a fitness expert; I'm just describing how this works for me.

———

Cognitive psychologists tell us that we all approach the world with a schema, a way of grouping things. Certain things always belong together; others never do. Constant creators have a greater capacity to associate ungrouped things and disassociate grouped ones. They regularly heed the advice of former president of Israel Shimon Peres, who suggested that when faced with two alternatives, we must immediately search for the third we haven't yet discovered.

According to author Kenneth Clark, this was one of the secrets of Leonardo da Vinci's unparalleled creativity. "To Leonardo," writes Clark, ". . . Rocks were not simply decorative silhouettes. They were part of the Earth's bones, with an anatomy of their own, caused by some remote seismic upheaval. Clouds were not random curls of the brush, drawn by some celestial artist, but were the congregation of tiny drops formed from the evaporation of the sea, and soon would pour back their rain into the rivers."

How to Think like Leonardo da Vinci author Michael Gelb concurs: "One secret of Leonardo's unparalleled creativity is his lifelong practice of combining and connecting disparate elements to form new patterns." Gelb cites Giorgio Vasari, who records an incident from Leonardo's childhood in which he was asked to paint a peasant's shield and subsequently "gathered and collected in his room an assortment of 'crawling reptiles, green lizards, crickets, snakes, butterflies, locusts, bats, and other strange species of this kind, and by adapting various parts of this multitude, he created a most horrible and frightening monster with poisonous breath that set the air on fire.'"

"Leonardo's dragons are a wonderful metaphor for his creative recipe of combination and connection. . . . On one page of his notebook Leonardo compares the rate and direction of travel of rays of light, the force of percussion, the voice of an echo, the lines of a magnet, and the movement of odor. . . . Leonardo's seriousness drove him to penetrate the essence of things, and his playfulness allowed him to make unprecedented, original connections."

Leonardo, explains Gelb, was driven to probe the "infinite

subtleties of nature," which ignited such incessant novelty and mystery that he was never without the spark of a new creation or innovation or exploration. In fact, da Vinci was so overwhelmed by the mysteries available to him, writes Serge Bramly, "he set aside his scalpel, compass, and pen and he took up his paintbrush once more."

When you make a habit out of defamiliarizing the ordinary, your life comes alive as the beautiful mystery, adventure, and frontier of possibility that it truly is—that it always has been. Along this frontier rise the sparks of your greatest creations, big and small.

6

STAY FOOLISH

I'm an artist and if you give me a tuba I'll bring you something out of it.

—**John Lennon**

THE SMARTER YOU ARE, THE HARDER IT IS TO SEE, UN-derstand, and create something new. It's the paradox of education. The greatest creators don't mind taking on something new. They never consider themselves fully educated. Many have little patience for traditional education. They're not looking to be the smartest or most praised or most degreed. They're aiming to keep igniting and keep learning. They never mind becoming an amateur again.

Amateurs are not afraid. They're in love, so to speak. They don't hesitate to do work that others think is a waste of time. They will try anything if it will teach them, inspire them, simplify them.

"The stupidest possible creative act is still a creative act," explains Clay Shirky in his book *Cognitive Surplus*. "On the spectrum of creative work, the difference between the mediocre and the good is vast. Mediocrity is, however, still on the spectrum; you can move from mediocre to good in increments. The real gap is between doing nothing and doing something."

Amateurs believe that creating something, even a rudimentary something, is better than creating nothing.

And they're right.

When you create, creativity becomes a constant—no matter how unqualified you are.

"Amateurs might lack formal training," writes Austin Kleon in his entertaining and insightful treatise *Show Your Work!* "but they're all lifelong learners." He points to *Infinite Jest* author David Foster Wallace who described good nonfiction as a chance to "watch somebody reasonably bright but also reasonably average pay far closer attention and think at far more length about all sorts of different stuff than most of us have a chance to in our daily lives."

"Amateurs fit the same bill," says Kleon. "They're just regular people who get obsessed by something and spend a ton of time thinking out loud about it." By far the most common place where creative sparks reside is any place where you can learn through action, even awkward, bumbling action. Being an amateur creator is not conceding that you'll never become a pro. Nor is it conceding that mediocre creations are the goal. It's conceding that to become a pro, and remain a pro, you have to remain willing to become a fool in love, again and again.

In his speech to the 2005 graduating class of Stanford, Steve Jobs explained what it has meant to him to remain foolish. He spoke about the promise his parents made to his birth mother—Jobs was adopted at birth—that he would go to college one day. When it was time to enroll, Jobs chose Reed College, a private liberal arts institution in Portland, Oregon, that, Jobs pointed out, was nearly as expensive as Stanford. His parents weren't wealthy and six months into his college career it became clear, at least to him, that it didn't make much sense to continue on the path and suck every penny from his working-class parents' savings. Jobs formally dropped out and began "dropping in on" classes that interested him. One of them was calligraphy. Reed offered one of the best courses in the country at the time.

Sleeping on friends' dorm floors and scraping by on every cent he could muster, Jobs dove into the class with no previous experience, only an honest interest. "I learned about serif and sans serif typefaces," he explained, "about varying the amount of space between different letter combinations, about what makes great typography great. It was beautiful, historical, artistically subtle in a way that science can't capture, and I found it fascinating."

None of it was practical at the time, Jobs admitted. But he enjoyed it and he learned from it. Then the ember of calligraphy know-how flickered to low heat as he took a greater interest in computers and programming. One of his early programming jobs, if you recall, was working a one-year stint as a contractor for Nolan Bushnell and Atari. Then one day the calligraphy came back to him as he and Steve Wozniak were designing the first Macintosh computer.

"We designed [the calligraphy] into the Mac," Jobs told the Stanford students. "It was the first computer with beautiful typography. If I had never dropped in on that single course in college, the Mac would have never had multiple typefaces or proportionally spaced fonts. And since Windows just copied the Mac, it's likely that no personal computer would have them."

It was a peculiar story to share with an audience full of students who had just completed one of the toughest undergrad paths a college student can take in this country. Especially given the lifetime of fascinating anecdotes Jobs had in his back pocket about success and failure and entrepreneurship and goals—the typical graduation speech fodder. But Jobs was making an important point and he needed an obscure, seemingly silly story to do it.

"When I was young," he continued, "there was an amazing publication called the *Whole Earth Catalog*, which was one of the bibles of my generation . . . created by a fellow named Stewart Brand. . . . This was in the late 1960s, before personal computers and desktop publishing, so it was all made with typewriters, scissors, and Polaroid cameras. . . . It was idealistic and overflowing with neat tools and great notions."

When the *Whole Earth Catalog* released its final issue in the 1970s, "I was your age," Jobs told the crowd. "On the back cover of their final issue was a photograph of an early morning country road, the kind you might find yourself hitchhiking on if you were so adventurous. Beneath it were the words: 'Stay Hungry. Stay Foolish.'

"I have always wished that for myself. And now . . . I wish that for you."

Constant creators hold tight to one constant, when all is falling apart and when all is thriving: foolishness. This is different from embracing the mind of a beginner who is willing to learn from anything. Foolishness is in the doing. It's an ability to embrace ideas, opportunities, and paths that we know are impractical and will break us down. Being foolish is doing what the majority would call stupid, senseless, or a waste of time.

To grind your sparks and spark your grind . . .
STAY FOOLISH

In his book *How Bad Do You Want It?* author Matt Fitzgerald describes a natural phenomenon that occurs when we are subjected to a scenario, often an adverse one, that requires us to relearn something from scratch—essentially, when we are subjected to becoming an amateur again. Fitzgerald calls the phenomenon the workaround effect.

He tells the story of Django Reinhardt, the legendary jazz player who was a virtuoso by the time he was eighteen years old. Later, a house fire badly burned the middle and ring fingers of his fret hand, leaving them paralyzed. He was forced to either put down his guitar and learn something else or learn how to play guitar all over again with eight fingers instead of ten. He chose the latter. The result was a new solo style that the music world called hot jazz. Critics judged Reinhardt's new style better than his original one. It was this style that he used to become a legend.

"The workaround effect comes in several flavors," explains Fitzgerald. "The flavor we're discussing here is known to scientists as neuroplasticity. The brain is highly plastic: It has almost unlimited ability to reorganize itself in response to roadblocks affecting its normal operations. For example, the brain of someone who loses her sight rewires itself in ways that sharpen the other senses."

He references a 2014 experiment by Anita Haudum of the University of Salzburg, who asked a group of runners to wear a pant leg of elastic tubing from the hip to the ankle to simulate an injury to that leg. The runners were obviously awkward at first but electromyography showed that because the tubing required greater muscle function, after seven weeks these runners showed greatly improved efficiency, not just with the tubing on but when they were allowed to run unrestrained. Fitzgerald explains, "This unconsciously learned new stride was not, in fact, visibly different from the subjects' natural stride, yet it was achieved through different patterns of brain and muscle activation. In effect, the subjects had found a new way to run the old way."

A similar but far more unfortunate thing happened to Willie Stewart when he was an eighteen-year-old recent high school grad working for a roofing company in Washington, D.C. The details are gruesome. He and a coworker were using a rope to clean off debris from an old roof they were replacing, when the rope inexplicably became wrapped around his arm. At the same time, the other end was pulled into a giant industrial fan. In an instant, the young man, a talented rugby player and a state champion wrestler, lost his arm.

Stewart sank into a depression following the accident, becoming

a shell of his former driven, athletic self. He spent most days in a recliner and most evenings partying. This was in the 1980s, an era when
resources for physically impaired athletes were not widely available.
He would have remained in this state if not for Julie Moss and the
1982 Ironman triathlon.

Stewart was in his recliner watching the coverage of the sporting
event when he witnessed Moss's now famous crawl across the finish
line in soiled shorts to finish second in the women's competition.

"Somewhere deep inside Willie, a flame was ignited," writes
Fitzgerald. "Feeling inspired (and impulsive), he immediately went
out and bought a white-and-red–striped one-piece Scott Tinley triathlon racing suit. He put it on and drove to Lake Elsa (now called
Lake Audubon), and dived in."

This was the beginning of a new life for Stewart as a triathlete.
He would have to relearn everything that once came naturally—
swimming with one arm, biking with one arm, and running with
one arm. But Stewart never looked back. In 1998, he qualified for the
Winter Paralympics in Nagano, Japan, and then, in 2002, he won a
silver medal in the Nordic relay.

But as Fitzgerald points out, his goal was never to compete against
disabled athletes. He wanted to compete against able-bodied ones, as
he once did. The same year he won the silver medal at the Paralympics, Stewart applied for the lottery of Ironman slots awarded each
year to disabled athletes and won one. A few months later he was in
Hawaii waiting for the starter's gun.

Stewart finished his first Ironman in 10:48:15, which won him
the disabled competition and placed him 532nd overall. It was only

the beginning. He completed the Ironman three more times and then moved on to other grueling races like a 100-kilometer trail run, 100-mile mountain bike races, and 24-hour adventure races. "In 2006," Fitzgerald writes, "Willie won the Catalina Marathon—not the disabled division or his age group but the whole race."

He explained, "As Willie Stewart discovered in learning how to ride a bike and to swim with one arm . . . it is impossible for an athlete faced with such a situation to consciously deduce how best to modify his technique and then programmatically acquire the new movement pattern. He must instead simply create and allow for opportunities to let it happen on its own."

There is clearly a distinct difference between traumatically losing a limb and being forced to relearn how to function, and remaining relatively healthy and trying something new. But the distinction is in the circumstances, not in the approach to learning.

This is why, when a friend or fan wonders aloud what Willie might have accomplished with both arms, Stewart always gives the same answer: "I wouldn't have done any of it."

Constant creators remain in a state of constant wonder. Not merely the kind of surreal wonder that can get stuck in fantasy if we're not careful. I'm talking about the kind of wonder that worries less about the whats and is more inclined to explore the what-ifs. And not just mentally explore. Physically explore. As a creator, you must lean into this. I learned this lesson on a bumpy road when I was first trying to become a professional speaker.

To be a top keynoter requires subject expertise, a physical presence, speaking skills, and the nerve to get up and talk in front of hundreds if not thousands of people. There was no reason to think that was a world in which I might excel. I'd never given a single talk. I'm also naturally shy—a classic introvert. Being around large groups of people was intimidating and draining. Then there was another fact. I was an absolute beginner at painting. There was no reason to think I'd be able to paint well on stage for a crowd, let alone fast. I hadn't even done it by myself, at my own house, over hours and hours.

The first person I confided in did his best to talk me out of it. He was a very well-known and successful corporate speaker who spoke sixty to seventy times a year and was in constant demand. He'd sacrificed his health for his craft, he admitted to me. He was basically exhausted. "Now you think it's sexy and glamorous," he told me. "But it's lonely, hard work. It's grueling. What can I do to convince you not to do this?"

There was nothing he could say to dampen my enthusiasm. His warnings didn't faze me. When he finally realized that I was all in no matter what he said, he shrugged his shoulders and I believe saw a little bit of himself as an amateur in me. He began to share a few nuggets of wisdom that helped me shape my concept.

"Speaking is five percent what you say," he explained, "and ninety-five percent how you say it. No one is going to remember anything about your presentation except the first ninety seconds and the last ninety seconds. Make them so spectacular, the ending so phenomenal, that the audience erupts."

He recommended not going to any speaking classes. Go and study U2, the Rolling Stones, Bruce Springsteen, live theater, and improv comedy, he advised. Go and learn how they actively engage an audience and then build a presentation and place actionable content in and around this experience.

The advice struck me as brilliant, and I took it to heart, but with a twist. I wanted to figure out how to extend ninety spectacular seconds to three minutes that built into a firecracker twelve-minute opening. Most speakers I'd seen opened with jokes or alarming facts to grab attention. What if I didn't say anything? What if, instead, I cranked up rock music and created a painting in ninety seconds flat?

There was a big problem with this idea. It was just an idea. I was, by every account imaginable, a fool. I couldn't paint anyone in an hour, let alone ninety seconds. But I knew instinctively that would be my innovation, my fire, something that had never been attempted on the professional speakers circuit. Looking back, the amazing thing was that I just threw myself into it. But I can see that the spark had been lit. Once I kept moving I was just fanning the flame. The more I moved, the more I progressed, the more that flame grew. And the more I learned.

I wasn't a painter, certainly had no keynote speaking skills, and I had no viable way of getting hired. I did know one critical thing from my knowledge of building a business. I needed to learn as much as I could as immediately as possible.

My first major step was to start rehearsing my talk. Nearly every day, I'd set my alarm for 4:00 A.M. and walk around my neighborhood like a nutcase, projecting my voice as if I were speaking in front of a large audience, waving my hands dramatically as I ran through ideas and stories that I had to connect into a coherent theme. I had to develop a fluency and cadence, and polish my story so well that I could do it backward and forward. The discipline of waking before anyone else was willing to wake felt inspiring.

To simulate the authentic feel of performing in front of thousands of people, I went to a local pastor and asked if I could borrow his stage from five to six in the morning three days during the workweek. Somewhat miraculously he gave me the keys to the sanctuary as long as I was cleared out by 6:00 A.M. The church seated four hundred people, which was an ideal setup. I needed to have this feeling of speaking to a crowd, and now three times a week I had my own stage and could speak to the hundreds of people I visualized. That was inspiring, arriving before dawn and running through my rough presentation. It got the fire growing bigger still.

When you're starting something totally new, you're taking a leap of faith. You have to believe, and you have to make other people believe, even when you're nowhere near ready. That's how I came up with the concept of my next step.

There's a Catch-22 in the keynote business. You can't get a good keynote without a history of keynotes. If you haven't done a keynote—ever—you have to find a way to create one. So I did what every early-stage entrepreneur does. I faked it.

Point Loma University had a free speakers' series. Perfect. I applied, got a spot, created a flier that made it sound like I had experience (which I did, just not in speaking), and then put them up all over the campus. Tasha and I asked all our friends to come in business attire so that we could guarantee a professional-looking audience. We hired three cameramen, and when the evening came we had a full crowd, including the pastor of the church where I'd been doing my predawn rehearsals.

How did it go?

It was an hour of sucking. I flailed like a fool and painted garbage. My ideas were disconnected and out of sync with the crowd. I was worried. But I was not deterred. What I lacked in talent, I made up for in passion. I was curious enough to keep trying and I was foolish enough not to quit. I wanted this to happen. I didn't quite have the rhythm down, but I was betting my family's diminishing financial security on the belief that if I kept at it, the know-how and the wow would come.

The bright future of anything—career, company, industry, relationship—relies on those who are willing to keep creating whether or not they've done it before, despite a lack of knowledge or resources. Stupidity and feelings of insufficiency can be fuel for innovation— often the most natural fuel you possess—if you let them be. Great creators don't spend as much time trying to discover their way to creativity as they do creating their way to discovery.

Like a child learning to draw, just draw. Stick figures if that's all you got. Don't try to be inspired. Don't trace or connect dots. Just create something. And then do it again. If you do it consistently enough, inspiration and discovery are guaranteed to occur. Get yourself used to acting forward, not merely thinking forward. And don't mind acting the fool. If you're going to stay on the creative edge, you regularly have to move before you're ready. Your friends and family will get used to it. Maybe they'll even be inspired.

"When someone has the insight to see clearly into the future," writes Peter Sims in *Little Bets*, "as Bill Gates did about the emerging computer industry . . . pursuing that brilliant vision with unwavering determination can produce remarkable results. However, when uncertainty replaces certainty or when we lack insight, experience, or expertise about problems, experimental innovation is a far better approach. . . . Most successful entrepreneurs, especially those who start businesses with limited capital, operate in this experimental way when trying new ideas. They think of learning the way most people think of failure."

Sims references the work of Saras Sarasvathy, a professor at the Darden Graduate School of Business at the University of Virginia. Sarasvathy studies what separates creative entrepreneurs from those who are more traditional. She looks primarily at how they make decisions and uses as an illustration of the difference the two different ways chefs cook a meal.

The first way, she says, "is for a chef to begin with a specific menu, pick out recipes, shop for the ingredients, and then cook the meal in their own, well-equipped kitchen." It's planned and procedural and therefore usually efficient.

However, says Sarasvathy, there's another way to prepare the meal. The chef simply steps into the kitchen without a menu or knowledge of all the available ingredients. The chef must rummage through the pantry and fridge to determine what's there and then begin piecing the meal together. "The result," explains the author, "might be great or it may not. The only certainty is that the outcome of the second approach will be less predictable than that of the first approach."

In other words, the way the second chef cooks the meal expands the spectrum of possibilities. This is what happens to your creative potential when you embrace the way of an amateur. Do it on a regular basis and your creative horizon keeps expanding.

Consider how Howard Schultz launched Starbucks. He intended to model the wonderful cafés he'd experienced in Italy, down to the menu items called by their Italian names. What he discovered was that American baristas found the bow ties awkward and customers complained about not comprehending the menu. So he took those shots in the face and morphed the experience.

Another famous company, Hewlett-Packard, began without its founders even having a firm vision of what they would produce. Talk about foolish. They came together and launched the venture because they wanted to work together. The how eventually came.

If there is a litmus test for engaging in foolish activity, it's fear. If you are truly acting on a spark that requires you to play the amateur, you will always fear something along the continuum from mild disappointment to complete disaster. However, the overlooked aspect of this sort of activity is that it is rarely a chore. Amateur spontaneity will stretch you, yes. But it is because you are stretched that this activity can be one of the most exhilarating and fulfilling things you do.

You have to act through the fear.

Ever jump off a cliff into a body of water? Even if you've done it numerous times, there is an element of fear that never leaves. But oh, the exhilaration you feel once you've done it far outweighs the fear beforehand. There is a reason the term "adrenaline junkie" exists. The feeling on the back side of these activities is addictive. In fact, being creatively foolish exposes you to a degree of delight you might not have experienced since the wonder years of your childhood, when all bets were off every day because no script had yet been written.

We are delighted by the sparks that rise from this sort of foolishness. We are drawn to their mystery. These sparks are fueled by our own natural curiosity.

Your logic tells you that your days are easiest when you know what to expect. There's truth in that. But your spirit reminds you that your days are only inspiring when you learn and stretch and grow. There's transcendence in the fascination of our own curiosity.

A long time ago I was reminded that the opposite of fear is not courage—it's faith. When faced with the many creative possibilities before you, your choice is to either move forward in faith, even foolish faith, or move backward in fear. And to do nothing is always moving backward. We long for growth and forward movement. Growth and comfort cannot coexist.

There is always fear in playing the fool. You are never fit for what you don't yet know and can't yet do. That's why great creators don't attempt to think their way into acting spontaneously. They just act spontaneously.

Sometimes the meal you prepare is garbage. Sometimes it's

heavenly. But you'll rarely have a shot at heavenly with a recipe in front of you.

There is a tendency to see creative foolishness as frivolous or even careless behavior. "You can't just drop everything," the logic goes, "and go on a wild-goose chase." This is a flawed view; it assumes that you are happy with your current "everything."

If you are, stay where you are and hold on to everything. Entertain nothing new. Learn no new thing. Spark no hidden potential.

If your everything isn't everything it's cracked up to be, let it go now and then to see what else you can learn and find.

In a piece for *Tech Insider*, science reporter Kelly Dickerson looks into the claim that astronaut Mark Watney (played by Matt Damon) makes in the film *The Martian* that NASA's Jet Propulsion Laboratory was founded after some Caltech students lit their dorm on fire with a rocket test gone wrong. Turns out, according to NASA's history archive, it's true. And it's a great illustration of what a few creative fools can accomplish.

In the mid-1930s, three graduate students—aerodynamics student Frank Malina, self-taught chemist Jack Parsons, and mechanic Ed Forman—set fire to their dorm room while testing a fueled rocket. Caltech promptly booted them off the campus. But they were fools in love. They kept testing.

They moved their operation into California's San Gabriel Mountains, calling themselves the "Suicide Club." Their first series of tests nearly affirmed the name as they lit the oxygen feed line on fire and it exploded around them, though fortunately no one was hurt. They kept at the seemingly foolish work and were eventually admitted back to Caltech, to which they responded by running more tests and being booted once and for all.

Over time, they became very proficient at building working models of rockets—without their exploding. But they were a fledgling operation until 1944, when their work was discovered and quickly sponsored by the U.S. Army "to develop rocket technology and the Corporal and Sergeant missile systems" in response to German V-2 rockets. The Suicide Club moved into an official lab in the foothills of Pasadena and united their team of experimenters under the name Jet Propulsion Laboratory, now known as simply JPL. This was fourteen years before the formation of NASA.

To date, JPL has been involved in over 125 NASA missions.

We can theorize all day long about theology, politics, creativity, and social change. But the rubber meets the road in practice, in actual encounter with real life. Too often our lives are small and circumscribed, structured to protect us from anything unfamiliar or unknown. We fight not to appear foolish. Stop fighting that fight. Let go of your self-consciousness and fear of humiliation. There are far greater things to lose than a little ego now and then.

While genius might reside in a spark, impact comes from grind. And sometimes you need to grind like a fool. Take consistent action whether you think it's leading you somewhere or not. In fact, sometimes it's better not to know where the path is heading. Plans rarely last long in their original form when you're constantly creating. As Mike Tyson says, "Everyone has a plan, until they get punched in the mouth."

You'll get punched in the face a lot when you're an amateur.

Which is why there's an important next step to taking action in an ill-informed, ill-prepared state. You don't just do and do and do. You must act on what you learn from your doing. Don't just get up and get punched in the same place again. You do to learn and then you apply it to grow your creative arsenal and output.

Sometimes, as in the case of Steve Jobs's calligraphy class, you don't immediately know what the point of the doing is. You did something because it interested you but there was no immediate application to your life. That's okay. It doesn't mean it was a waste. And there's no need to force the lesson or contrive one. Your mind will clarify the ties for you the more new experiences you take on. As you grow older, you will find that none of these experiences has been a waste.

The majority of your amateur experiences, your foolish experiments, will teach you something right away and illuminate an immediate application to a current venture. This application must be captured. You must become proficient at refining your creativity through reaction.

While I spend time in my studio practicing my performance of every painting and while I continue to study art history and technique, I don't aim to trace the academic rules of great art with my finished work. I am not creating a product to be hung in a museum and praised by curators and art critics for decades to come. I am creating a product to evoke feelings that will compel you to take bolder, more innovative, more authentic actions today. I don't need three months or three years to create something that makes that sort of impact. I need three minutes. You may need even less time.

The standards of creativity in the real world are not the same as they are at the Louvre or at Sotheby's. To be more innovative, to be a greater creative asset in every role you play, you do not need ideas that will be lauded by economists and MBA students for the next century. You need a place to start. One idea is all it takes.

Constant creators work with a continuous sense of urgency to raise the bar in every facet of their lives. They resist hitting the cruise control when something is working. And they rarely rely on existing road maps to direct future paths because they know the best road map is an ever-increasing awareness.

If you can begin to see creativity through this lens—accelerated output, immediate impact—you will begin to see why acting the fool matters. The simplest definition of great art is that it engages and inspires. Waiting for the right idea to act is a cop-out. You don't need the perfect idea. You just need a decent one and a penchant for constant progress. You're only fooling yourself if you think patience is the path to more creativity.

You don't need brilliance to make creative progress. You just need enough foolish drive to move forward when you are neither qualified nor equipped. Opportunities come quicker and steadier when you forget your ego and just go.

Certain writers throughout history believed you could only create one great book in your lifetime. Certain painters throughout history believed a similar thing about paintings. On one hand, I understand this view. If I were going to create my life masterpiece—the one product that would embody my best skills, spirit, and persona, and establish my legacy for all of time—I would take some time working on it. I wouldn't stand on a stage and paint it in three minutes.

But on the other hand, I am not looking to create one single product and I don't agree that it's all we have to offer. Our lives are our greatest product. When the sparks are flying every day a lot can happen: a life of insane vibrancy and joy and impact. A lot you could have never dreamt up in your most lucid moments. So I look to create as many sparks as possible. I accelerate to scale my impact and increase the likelihood of a breakthrough idea. Instead of spending all my time mapping out my masterpiece, I paint for the trash can quite often.

This isn't my way of bowing out of maximum effort. And it's not my way of trying to preempt the rejection of buyers or critics who might say my art doesn't stand up to museum standards. It is my way of creating a lab in which I am not limited by flawlessness or expectation. If what I paint is for the trash can, I am free to rapidly explore, dream, and discover without the traditional risk of failure.

Progress requires making strides. Where creativity is concerned, the shorter the stride, the greater the progress. And short strides are full of stumbles. Don't buy into the notion that you can take a giant leap if you spend enough time strategizing. It's as much a play to avoid looking stupid as it is trying to actually succeed. Besides, by the time you polish your smart plan, creative fools will have lapped you twice.

Opt instead to just go and make the sparks fly. Try something new every week—walk up to a stranger and strike up a conversation, take interest in his or her life. Learn something new every year—take on a new language or study a new subject. You will look foolish at times. But you will learn more in this posture than if you kept doing what you know. And along the way, you will learn to love learning. As you learn you will refine your skills, rekindle adventure, and ignite creativity more frequently than you knew you could.

Don't fear the fool in you. Let him lead you into creative frontiers every day.

7

FALL IN LOVE

The creative mind plays with the object it loves.

— Carl Jung, *The Collected Works of C. G. Jung*

"**E**VEN ON HER DEATHBED," WRITES BARBARA GOLD-smith of Madame Curie, "Marie had insisted that a dose of fresh air might be all that was needed to help her recover. With the persistence that had allowed her to perform seemingly impossible tasks, Marie Curie never acknowledged that her beloved radium might have betrayed her."

Goldsmith points out that in Curie's autobiography, the great scientist admitted that radiation had damaged her health only slightly, in a minor way. Even when she was a little older and constantly bothered by humming in her ears and deteriorating eyesight, in a letter to a friend she only acknowledged, "Perhaps radium has something to do with these troubles, but it cannot be affirmed with certainty."

Madame Curie, for all intents and purposes, was very protective of her work. And while the knowledge of radiation in the early 1900s had not, as she insisted, yet affirmed the direct link between exposure and major health problems, Curie would likely not have admitted it if such were the case. And it was the case come 1925, explains Goldsmith. "At wooden tables in the U.S. Radium Corporation factory in New Jersey a row of young women sat painting luminous numbers on watch dials, diligently licking their brushes to bring them to a fine point. The paint contained only one part radium per six-hundred thousand parts of inert substances, yet within three years, fifteen young women perished as radium poisoning destroyed their jaws and bone marrow."

History now knows with certainty that it was exposure to radiation that killed not only Madame Curie, but her daughter Irène and son-in-law Frédéric, who won the Curie family's third Nobel Prize. How could they not have seen it? asks Goldsmith. "The answer, I believe, was love," she answers. "It prevented Marie and Pierre from seeing radium with the same cold, scientific eye they brought to their other work. Even as they warned of the dangers of radium exposure, at their bedside the Curies had kept a vial of radium salts to observe its beautiful glow before falling asleep. Marie referred to radium as 'my child.'"

Love drives us to make great sacrifices. Personal sacrifices. Even the ultimate sacrifice.

It is easy to look at iconic creators like Martin Luther King Jr. or

Abraham Lincoln or Marie Curie or Mother Teresa and conclude they are rare individuals, one of a handful in a generation, with an extraordinary bent toward serving others. I don't want to diminish the value of the world-changing service of such people—but I think it's doing them a great disservice to say it was all about the doing for them. Yes, they served in a way few in history did. But they didn't do it only for altruistic reasons. There was something in it for them, too.

They also did it because they loved their art. They loved the unique canvas and tools they had within them. And they loved the pictures these created, pictures that inspired and instructed and offered a window into something better for others. So they absorbed themselves into this work with all their being. It wasn't about legacy. It wasn't about money or accolades or early retirement. They were in love with their art—the manifestation of their being, and the proof of their becoming. It was this love that drove them to change the world with their creativity.

To grind your sparks and spark your grind . . .
FALL IN LOVE

"A writer looking for subjects," says Annie Dillard, "inquires not after what he loves best, but after what he alone loves at all." This distinct and deep love of your creations is the furnace of your existence. It ignites you to generate sparks and grind them day after day.

When you learn to trust the creative process, attach yourself to your work, keep your day job, embrace a routine, defamiliarize the ordinary, and stay foolish, creativity becomes a love affair. And when you're hooked, you're hooked for life.

You're obsessed.

A little crazy.

Mad.

And that's the kind of relationship you're meant to have with creativity.

That sort of relationship is why Wade Davis has spent much of his life studying and living with indigenous communities in Latin America, where, according to *Time* magazine, "he has created more than 6,000 plant species."

It's why photographer Robbie Shone has spent the last decade capturing images of the world's deepest, darkest, longest cave systems, spending as long as four days in the Earth's belly at a time.

It's why Sylvia Earle has spent the last fifty years exploring the Earth's oceans and fighting to protect them. She's eighty years old today and still donning her scuba gear and diving deep. "Every time I slip into the ocean," she said, "it's like going home."

And it's why Tommy Caldwell and Kevin Jorgeson ground through more than seven years and two failed attempts to give free-climbing Yosemite's Dawn Wall one more try. "Most of the days of the year," explained Caldwell in the days leading up to the attempt, "I wake up with this on my mind, thinking, What am I going to do today to get one step closer? It gets me outside every day in the mountains in beautiful places, pushing myself. It makes me live at a higher level, having this as part of my life."

On January 14, 2015, as the sun set in Yosemite National Park, thirty-six-year-old Caldwell and thirty-year-old Jorgeson completed their climb, widely considered the most difficult free ascent (using ropes only to catch falls) in the history of rock climbing. To do it, the pair ate, slept, and relieved themselves hanging from the sheer granite face of a behemoth rock formation for nine straight days, climbing 3,000 vertical feet along widely spaced holds, many as narrow as half an inch.

The duo climbed mostly at night, for six-hour stints, to keep sweaty palms at a minimum. For the remaining eighteen hours each day, they rested in a tent that hung from the face—it was rigged with rope and webbing to keep it upright—and repaired the splitting skin on their fingertips with a combination of beeswax and oil.

Halfway through the climb, Jorgeson struggled with the most difficult pitch of the climb. It took him seven days and ten attempts to finally make it past and continue the climb with Caldwell, who was waiting patiently for him to succeed.

A week later they'd done it. The climbers reached the top and were greeted by more than seventy friends, family, and onlookers who'd hiked eight miles up the back of the mountain. Hundreds more cheered from the valley floor 3,000 feet below.

After the hugs and the sprays of bubbly, the climbers spoke to the *New York Times*.

"What do you hope this does for climbing?" asked the *Times*.

"I would love for this to open people's minds to what an amazing sport this is," beamed Caldwell. "I think the larger audience's conception is that we're thrill seekers, out there for an adrenaline rush. We really aren't at all. It's about spending our lives in these beautiful places and forming these incredible bonds with friends and family. It's really a lifestyle. . . . And if that love can spread, that's really a great thing."

"When the climber Warren Harding reached the top of the Dawn Wall in 1970," according to the *New York Times*, "and was asked why he did it, he said, 'Because we're insane!' Why did you do it?"

"These days it seems like everything is padded and comes with warning labels," said Caldwell. "This just lights a fire under me, and that's a really exciting way to live. And this has driven me for a really long time."

When you fall in love with your unique brand of creativity, strange things happen.

You've been there before. You've fallen in love. What happens?

It's difficult to describe.

"Earlier times may not have understood it any better than we do," confesses Susan Neiman in *Moral Clarity*, "but they weren't as embarrassed to name it: the life force or spark . . . it's something that makes those who have it fully human, and those who don't look like sleepwalkers. . . ."

When we're in a love affair with creativity, details like time and space begin to fade into meaninglessness. Being together is tantamount. We don't care where we're sitting together or whether any words are spoken. Being united is imperative, wherever that is.

During Jane Austen's most productive years, it was in the family parlor, with her mother sewing nearby and the constant obligation of visitors. She wrote on small pieces of paper that could easily be stuffed in a drawer or under a book.

For Agatha Christie, it was anywhere she could find a stable surface to bear her typewriter. She didn't even own a desk.

For the apostle Paul, it was often in Roman prisons. There he wrote many of his letters to the early Christian churches.

For Martin Luther King Jr., too, it was in a prison cell in Birmingham, Alabama, or on the Edmund Pettus Bridge in Selma, or the steps of the Lincoln Memorial in Washington, D.C.

For Annie Dillard, it was in a glorified outhouse on an island in Washington's Puget Sound. She called it a windowless shed. With no electricity, which meant no heat, which meant to get heat she had to get wood, which wasn't for sale on the remote island, which meant she had to chop it herself, with no previous experience cutting wood. And did I mention it was winter? There in her love shack, she and her creativity pecked out the Pulitzer Prize–winning *Pilgrim at Tinker Creek*.

For many musicians, their first love shack was a garage: the Ramones, Nirvana, Creedence Clearwater Revival, and the Who, to name a small sampling.

Many companies also found garages, sometimes not even their own garages, to suit their love affair just fine. According to *Inc.* magazine, there are at least five $25 billion ones: Google, Apple, Microsoft, Amazon, and Disney.

The list goes on of great creators who pursued their love affair with creativity regardless of their current circumstances.

Why?

Because the smaller details don't matter when you're in love. Being together is it.

When she was still in her home country of Thailand, Hong Thaimee held a well-paying job as a marketing manager for the pharmaceutical giant Merck. Before that she'd been a spokesmodel and TV personality for Singha Beer. In Bangkok, a city of socioeconomic extremes, she was on the wealthy side of the spectrum. She was an MBA-holding, gainfully employed professional for a major company. She was also frequently recognized on the streets. While the titles and recognition massaged her ego, none of it melted her heart. Thaimee's true love arose from her upbringing in Chiang Mai, a much smaller and more communal city in northern Thailand, where farm-fresh food was available year-round and her grandmother's uncanny cooking ability had always spoken to her soul.

No one but she and a few close friends knew the extent of her love, which is why most of her coworkers were shocked when she traded her life in Bangkok for an obscure and modest life in New York City to chase the outlandish dream of opening a Thai restaurant in Manhattan. Living with an American friend and without any experience in the restaurant industry, she walked into Spice Market, the celebrated restaurant of famous chef and restaurateur Jean-Georges Vongerichten, to ask for a job. When the restaurant manager noted Thaimee's experience on her résumé he was puzzled. What was her interest in working there, of all places? The kitchen, she told him. She wanted to work her way into the kitchen. The manager said, "Let's see," and he hired her on the spot—as a hostess. If she was going to work in the famous kitchen of Jean-Georges, she was going to have to earn her place.

Two months into the job and on her break at work, Thaimee was eating a bowl of pad Thai that she'd prepared at home—her grandmother's special recipe. The manager happened on her and asked where she got the food. It smelled delicious.

"I made it," Thaimee explained, and the manager asked for a bite.

Thaimee obliged and the manager's eyes widened as the food hit his palate. He insisted she make the same dish for Jean-Georges the following night. He will be here, the manager explained, and he would want to taste this.

The world-renowned chef tasted Thaimee's meal the following night and immediately moved her to his kitchen. She wouldn't be allowed to cook, however. She had to start out by plating food.

Thaimee was grateful but not deterred. She went out and bought a chef's coat and a top-end set of knives. She loved being around food every day but working in someone else's kitchen wasn't her goal. Her love wouldn't be fully manifest until she could prepare and serve her own food for others to enjoy. "Thai food was popular back then," she explains, "but it wasn't refined and lacked real heart. I knew I could offer something better that what was being served."

It would take eighteen more months and work in the kitchens of two more Jean-Georges restaurants, but Thaimee's relentless desire to open a restaurant finally persuaded some investors to take a chance. In 2011, she opened Ngam (pronounced "nom") in the East Village of Manhattan, which features a large neon sign on one of the walls that reads LOVE and an open kitchen so she and her employees can interact with diners throughout each night.

"That's all I've wanted to do," Thaimee explained. "Love people and lift them up with good food. When people come to Ngam, I want them to know that no matter what they're going through, no matter what kind of day they've had, they will be loved here."

Thaimee's love hasn't gone unnoticed. By 2013, less than two years after she opened her doors, the *Village Voice* named Ngam the best Thai restaurant not just in the East Village but in all of New York City. It was an astonishing honor for such a new restaurant in a city known globally for its food culture. Thaimee's reputation hasn't diminished either. In 2014, she competed against Bobby Flay on *Iron Chef America* and the following year released a cookbook, *True Thai*, that was featured in every Williams-Sonoma store nationwide.

"It wasn't easy," Thaimee admits now, "but I was following my heart and I always knew that even if I didn't succeed I would have no regrets. And I would just find another way to show my love."

———

A new creator will fall into the temptation of trying to orchestrate the perfect space and time to start creating, but that only impedes progress. He doesn't yet understand love. He's like the freshman trying to impress the girl with a two-hundred-dollar dinner when all she wants is a burger and a good chat. Or like the woman named Martha who was busy washing the dishes while Jesus was talking with her sister. The first-century physician named Luke describes the scene:

> As Jesus and his disciples were on their way, he came to a village where a woman named Martha opened her home to him. She had a sister called Mary, who sat at the Lord's feet

listening to what he said. But Martha was distracted by all the preparations that had to be made. She came to him and asked, "Lord, don't you care that my sister has left me to do the work by myself? Tell her to help me!" "Martha, Martha," the Lord answered, "you are worried and upset about many things, but few things are needed—or indeed only one. Mary has chosen what is better, and it will not be taken away from her."

When there's love, creators no longer wrestle with the wheres and whens. The real matter at hand is the pursuit of the next creation, the next opportunity to display their love. When Liz Powers was a freshman at Harvard, she followed her heart for the homeless and began working in shelters in the Boston area. In a *New York Times* article, Powers explains she "was flipping pancakes and making eggs at 6:30 in the morning . . . but I didn't really get to know anyone." A year later, she joined LIFT, a nonprofit organization that equipped her with practical tools for working with homeless people.

The more time she spent with homeless and disenfranchised people, the more she noted how lonely many of them were and the more her heart longed for a solution to meet this need. At the very least, how could she create a safe place for them to support each other? That's when it hit her. Perhaps she could marry two of her passions into one. This became the spark of something much bigger, though she didn't know what just yet.

"Having been an artist," explains *New York Times* writer Glenn

Rifkin, "[Powers] urged local shelters to create art groups where their residents could come together, make art, and earn one another's trust. With a public service fellowship from Harvard, she spent a year working on her concept."

In the context of these groups, the flame of Powers's idea grew, namely because she noted the incredible abilities of some of the participants. They were truly gifted artists. This discovery caused her to ask the biggest question of all: How could she help their work find a greater audience? Powers believed people would pay for it and she wondered if that just might give them a way out of their situations.

She spent her time piecing together art shows in local churches. While the artwork featured was good, the local response was underwhelming. She wasn't deterred. When a space in a local shopping mall was donated to her, she constructed a more permanent art show that garnered the attention of dozens of shoppers. "When is the next show?" they asked.

Powers's initial spark was now a legitimate fire that others noticed. Her heart for the homeless was an inspiration and those who learned of what she was doing wanted in. Powers brought in her brother to help her discern how to best scale the distribution of the homeless artists' work. ArtLifting was born—an online portal to celebrate and sell the artwork of homeless and disabled artists.

When ArtLifting.com launched, it featured the work of only four artists and sold only through e-commerce. Within weeks, however, the artists had earned thousands of dollars and ArtLifting was a national media story. Today, the Web site features the artwork of seventy-two artists from eleven states and has tripled its distribution channels to include licensing and corporate purchasing options, already boasting clients like Microsoft and Staples. Most recently, Powers raised more than $1 million from twenty venture capitalists and angel investors, including Blake Mycoskie, the founder of TOMS Shoes, the first company to create a massively successful enterprise by giving away one product (a pair of shoes) to someone in need for every product sold. If anyone knows the value of a heart-first approach to creativity, it's Mycoskie. And Powers is proving the path once again.

When you don't know where to find creative inspiration, it's often because you're not listening to your heart. From it, said King Solomon, "flow the springs of life." Creativity lives in your heart. And because that's true, you can ignite sparks and grind them anywhere—from beige cubicles to the streets of India to the middle row of a rented light-blue minivan, which is where a friend once wrote for a week to meet a book deadline while his own car, and office roof, were simultaneously being repaired.

Clearly, this sort of love gets messy now and then.

Freelance writer and neuroscientist Andrew Tate writes that on the day Einstein died, *Time* photographer Ralph Morse ditched the crowds gathered at Princeton Hospital and found his way to Einstein's office at the Institute for Advanced Study, where he snapped a photo of Einstein's desk. "Not an inch of Einstein's desk is free of paper. Books, manuscripts, magazines, and envelopes are everywhere (along with what looks like a cookie jar). The same goes for the shelves. One shelf holds neatly arrayed journals, but elsewhere are piles and piles of papers. It's a mess, and he liked it that way."

Twain, Jobs, Zuckerberg, and Tony Hsieh also had or have uber-messy work environments. Clearly a few fanned piles of paper, an old lunch sack, and a half-eaten apple won't come between these great creators and their creativity.

But don't take this too far. There's a place for clean and tidy, too. The love affairs of some creators thrive in such environments. The point isn't that messy means more creativity. Or that tidy does either. Messy or tidy is more a personality trait or preference than a principle. The point is that when you're in love with creativity, you don't worry about either. You take it as it comes each day. And the two of you get down to creating right away.

The most profound element of this sort of love—of any true love—is that you always have each other.

In good times, sparks and champagne spray the air. Life is artful and meaningful and a true manifestation of who you are.

And in bad times—in loss, rejection, disappointment—creativity is still there, reminding you that an upswing is just a spark away. When you have creativity, you have the ultimate bond.

There's an ancient Japanese story about a Sakai tea man who was perusing the wares of a street market. Suddenly, his eyes caught sight of a Chinese tea jar so beautiful he thought nothing of the cost and bought it. So pleased was he with his discovery that he invited the famed tea man Sen no Rikyū to a gathering with friends to show off the beautiful piece. But when the Sakai man served the tea, Rikyū didn't give the jar a second glance.

Greatly disappointed, the Sakai man tossed the jar against a wall, where it shattered into pieces. Then he left it and went to bed.

Unbeknownst to him, two friends had heard the crash from outside and came back in to find the jar fragments on the ground. They gathered them up and took them home, where they mended the jar.

The same two friends then invited Sen no Rikyū to another gathering of their own, where they offered him tea in the mended jar. When Rikyū saw the jar he exclaimed, "That piece is magnificent!"

The friends had not mended the jar with glue or paste or the typical bond of that day. They had pieced the jar back together with liquid gold.

Many link this story to the birth of kintsugi, an ancient Japanese art that translates to "patch with gold." Kintsugi artists take broken pieces of ceramics and pottery and put them back together using gold lacquer. The end product is more striking than when it was first finished.

This is what it's like to have creativity by your side.

What is broken or fallen or shattered in pieces can be made more beautiful. And the truth is that you and I have already been broken, we've fallen, we've been shattered before. The scars we bear tell our stories, our individual stories.

Pop culture often tells us to hide the scars and fissures and cracks. Put on the shimmer and shine. The right rings and crowns and colored robes. So we all look . . . acceptable . . . famous . . . Instagram worthy . . . the same.

The art of kintsugi offers a different view: vessels are stronger and more magnificent and more creative because they have imperfection, not because they are without them. Your cracks, fault lines, and unique contours are where your gold resides. Love your eccentricities as creativity does. See them for what they truly are—the distinct tools of your creative trade. Deploy them with adoration, gratitude, and great pride. Your best works will come alive.

And so will you.

In the end, creating is as human as breathing.

You breathe in. You breathe out. This proves you are living.

You absorb. You create. This proves you are alive.

You are a human being, and a human becoming. Your creativity fashions the bridge between the two.

Who are you? Who will you become?

Who you are is art. Do nothing and you still embody a masterpiece.

But you are more than a marble statue. Your world is more than a museum. You are organic and meant to manifest the features of your becoming.

Your becoming is beautiful and lucid. It inspires and instructs.

Your becoming is also hideous and chaotic. It inflames and confounds.

Thus, your life sings both magic and mystery. Fulfillment and frustration.

Thus, the products of your becoming are risky.

Don't let the risk confine you. Being without becoming is riskier still.

Let your senses craft substance; your mind, meaning; your heart, belief. Allow the combinations to originate emotion; let conviction be fashioned. Desire and despair. Satisfaction and discontent. Faith. Hope. Love.

Do it every day.

Creations will rise from your lips, feet, and the tips of your fingers.

"Know thine opportunity," Pittacus said.

Creativity is your greatest opportunity.

Pursue it like a lover you can't live without.

In the end, what you truly love determines who you become. But knowing what you truly love is challenging to clarify . . . until you're in a difficult or desperate situation. Love is often theoretical until there is no longer time or energy for theories. That's when your lens is in clear focus. And it's when you know where you stand with creativity.

When I was thirty years old, without a company or job or stream of income, one thing I knew for sure was that I loved my wife and our three boys. While I wanted to uncover a new career that mattered to me, that made sense with my experience, I would have gone door-to-door asking if neighbors needed their lawns mowed to ensure my family's needs were met. My love for them lit a fire under me to forget myself and forge ahead, no matter what it took.

If you'd have asked me what else I loved back then, I would have struggled to pinpoint anything I loved that definitively or deeply. In truth, I loved the idea of a lot of things: success, hard work, serving other people. It wasn't that I didn't believe in those things. I did. But love and belief are two different forces. Both are strong and significant in our lives, but I understand now that I can believe in something and not love it. However, I cannot truly love something and not believe in it. Love in action is the ultimate proof of the depth of our beliefs.

How deeply do you believe in creativity?

I had little faith in it during the course of my first career. I treated it like a one-night stand. I had no interest in a long-term relationship; I just wanted my needs met. A relationship with creativity wasn't part of my belief system. I had more important things to love.

Today it's different. Perhaps it's more accurate to say I'm different. I was forced back to creativity's door, and in my desperation I had an honest reckoning not only with myself but with my relationship with creativity. That's when I began to see what I'd been missing, and why creativity deserved my love each day.

Today, rather than going to creativity only when I have a need I can't meet with hard work, I wake up with creativity next to me. I walk hand in hand with creativity throughout the day. And when I lie down at night, creativity is still by my side.

Don't get me wrong; I'm still working at the relationship, and you will, too, as you strengthen this newfound love. I still have a default tendency to grind blindly. I don't know that it will ever go away. But because I've worked at my relationship with creativity constantly and consistently each day, creativity nudges me when I'm being detached or shortsighted or forgetful. I need this. You need this.

Because it is not just a reminder of the need to feed the relationship. It is ultimately a reminder to follow the brightest path, make the best progress, and be and become the best you. That's the best kind of love.

NOTES

Chapter 0: Creativity Is a Complicated Friend

4 **public companies spend on innovation:** PricewaterhouseCoopers, Strategy&, "2015 Global Innovation 1000: Innovation's New World Order," October 2015, www.strategyand.pwc.com/media/file/2015 -Global-Innovation-1000-Fact-Pack.pdf.

12 **his own writings:** James Gleick, *Isaac Newton* (New York: Vintage, 2003), 55.

13 **"world's paramount mathematician":** Ibid., 34.

17 **best approach to life:** Ecclesiastes 3:9–14 (New International Version).

17 **"We are born makers":** Brené Brown, *Rising Strong* (New York: Spiegel & Grau/Random House, 2015), 7.

Chapter 1: Trust the Process

25 **"The traveller sees":** G. K. Chesterton. *The Autobiography of G. K. Chesterton* (San Francisco: Ignatius Press, 2006), 306.

27 **"most virile moment"**: Federico Fellini and Charlette Chandler, *I, Fellini* (New York: Cooper Square Press, 2001), 83, 85.

28 **"devoutly ethical approach"**: Kirk Curnutt, *Coffee with Hemingway* (London: Duncan Baird, 2007), 16.

30 **"ever taken a shower"**: Nolan Bushnell and Gene Stone, *Finding the Next Steve Jobs: How to Find, Hire, Keep and Nurture Creative Talent* (New York: Simon & Schuster, 2013), 224.

31 **"does not follow ideas"**: Nolan Bushnell, "Nolan Bushnell Intro Speaking Video," accessed November 10, 2016, www.nolanbushnell.com.

32 **"wasn't $200 million"**: Alexis C. Madrigal, "Chuck E. Cheese's, Silicon Valley Startup: The Origins of the Best Pizza Chain Ever," *Atlantic*, July 17, 2013, www.theatlantic.com/technology/archive/2013/07/chuck-e-cheeses-silicon-valley-startup-the-origins-of-the-best-pizza-chain-ever/277869.

33 **"when I'm not crying"**: Walter Isaacson, *Steve Jobs* (New York: Simon & Schuster, 2011), 75.

34 **($4.4 billion in stock)**: Eric Slivka, MacRumors, March 10, 2011, www.macrumors.com/2011/03/10/steve-jobs-ranked-worlds-110th-richest-person-with-net-worth-of-8-3-billion.

36 **"highly correlated with creativity"**: Scott Barry Kaufman and Carolyn Gregoire, *Wired to Create* (New York: TarcherPerigee, 2015), 28.

37 **"Dr. Kaufman's research"**: Christie Aschwanden, "'Wired to Create' Shows the Science of a Messy Process," *New York Times*, February 8, 2016, www.nytimes.com/2016/02/09/science/book-review-wired-to-create-scotty-barry-kaufman-carolyn-gregoire.html?ribbon-ad-idx=8&rref=books&_r=2.

37 **"staying loose"**: Ibid.

38 **"creative magic happens"**: Ibid.

40 **"if you ask a"**: Annie Dillard, *The Writing Life* (New York: HarperPerennial, 1990), 70, 71.

40 **"never be solvable"**: Bruce Grierson, "Eureka!," *Psychology Today*, March 9, 2015, www.psychologytoday.com/articles/201503/eureka.

47 **"little bets help us":** Peter Sims, *Little Bets* (New York: Simon & Schuster, 2013), 21.

48 **"bent tip of a grassblade":** Dillard, *The Writing Life*, 74–75.

49 **jellyfish into windows:** Jenn Savedge, "9 Young Inventors Who May Just Save the World," Mother Nature Network, October 20, 2014, www .mnn.com/green-tech/research-innovations/blogs/9-young-inventors -who-may-just-save-the-world.

50 **"insatiably curious approach":** Michael J. Gelb, *How to Think like Leonardo da Vinci* (New York: Random House, 2009), 37.

50 **"he raised continuous doubts":** Ibid., 102.

50 **"he had no passion":** Daniel J. Boorstin, *The Creators* (New York: Vintage, 1993), 915.

50 **"pure quest for truth":** Gelb, *How to Think like Leonardo da Vinci,* 102.

51 **"the true mistress":** Ibid., 145.

52 **"My growth," he writes:** Josh Waitzkin, *The Art of Learning* (New York: Simon & Schuster, 2009), xvii.

53 **"enjoyment of the process":** Ibid., 29.

54 **"As a writer," asks:** Steven Pressfield, *The Authentic Swing* (n.p.: Black Irish Entertainment, 2013), 74.

54 **"fullness and evacuation":** Pablo Picasso, quoted in Alfred H. Barr, Jr. ed., *Picasso: Forty Years of His Art* (New York: The Museum of Modern Art, 1939), 17–18.

56 **"To all viewers":** David Bayles and Ted Orland, *Art & Fear* (n.p.: Image Continuum, 1993), 5.

56 **"The key element":** Mihaly Csikszentmihalyi, *Flow* (New York: HarperPerennial, 2008), 67.

57 **"Teaching children in order":** Ibid.

58 **"Curry transcended the game":** Al Saracevic, "Stephen Curry Authors a Signature Moment," *San Francisco Chronicle*, February 28, 2016, www.sfchronicle.com/sports/article/Stephen-Curry-authors-his -signature-moment-6859193.php.

58 **"needs to stop it"**: Tweet, @KingJames, 8:34 P.M., February 27, 2016, mobile.twitter.com/KingJames/status/7038004659858.

58 **"Far below NBA standard"**: "30—Stephen Curry," NBAdraft.net, www.nbadraft.net/players/stephen-curry.

59 **"an extreme outlier"**: Drake Baer, "Steph Curry Literally Sees the World Differently Than You Do," *New York Magazine*, June 13, 2016, nymag.com/scienceofus/2016/06/steph-curry-perception-performance.html.

59 **"feel more creative"**: Drake Baer, "NBA Star Steph Curry Talks Daily Routine, Sensory-Deprivation Tanks, and Hacking His Brain," *Tech Insider*, February 1, 2016, www.techinsider.io/steph-curry-interview-on-basketball-life-championships-2016-2.

61 **"based on the ancient techniques"**: Benj Edwards, "Who Needs GPS? The Forgotten Story of Etak's Amazing 1985 Car Navigation System," *Fast Company*, June 26, 2015, www.fastcompany.com/3047828/who-needs-gps-the-forgotten-story-of-etaks-amazing-1985-car-navigation-system.

64 **prescribed burning actually enhanced:** David J. Augustine, Justin D. Derner, and Daniel G. Milchunas, "Prescribed Fire, Grazing, and Herbaceous Plant Production in Shortgrass Steppe," *Rangeland Ecology & Management* 63, no. 3 (May 2010): 317–23.

Chapter 2: Attach Yourself to the Work

66 **"It is not what"**: Richard Friedenthal, *Letters of the Great Artists from Blake to Pollock* (London: Thames and Hudson, 1963), 259.

66 **"Know your own bone"**: Robert Frost, quoted in Annie Dillard, *The Writing Life* (New York: HarperPerennial, 1990), 68.

67 **"made painting go astray"**: Pablo Picasso, quoted in Marius de Zayas, "Picasso Speaks," *The Arts*, May 1923, 315–26.

68 **"far more marvelous"**: Julia Cameron, *The Right to Write* (New York: Tarcher/Putnam, 1998), 84.

68 **"glimpses a destination"**: Frederick Buechner, *Listening to Your Life* (New York: HarperCollins, 1992), 168.

69 **"They are driven by a":** William Zinsser, *On Writing Well* (New York: HarperPerennial, 2016), 5.

70 **case for detachment:** Gill Corkindale, "Detach Yourself from Your Work," *Harvard Business Review,* January 28, 2011, hbr.org/2011/01 /detach-yourself-from-your-work.

72 **"Work? I never worked":** Quotes in the following order: Ernie Banks, "'Let's play two!' Ernie Banks' words reflected his outlook on life," *Fox Sports,* January 24, 2015, www.foxsports.com/mlb/story/chicago-cubs -hall-of-famer-ernie-banks-dies-at-83-great-quotes-lets-play-two -012315; Ray Bradbury, "Ray Bradbury gives talk at UCLA," *Daily Bruin,* April 9, 1998, dailybruin.com/1998/04/09/ray-bradbury-gives-talk-at -ucl; Thomas Edison, "Famous Quotations from Thomas Edison," www .thomasedison.org/index.php/education/edison-quotes.

72 **"compartmentalizing our work and home":** Christian Jarrett, "Work/ Life Separation Is Impossible. Here's How to Deal with It," *99U,* 99u.com /articles/31721/worklife-separation-is-impossible-heres-how-to-deal -with-it.

73 **"only a rumor":** Cited in Brené Brown, *Rising Strong* (New York: Spiegel & Grau/Random House, 2015), 7.

74 **"love Mike Webster":** Jeanne Marie Laskas, *Concussion* (New York: Random House, 2015), 14.

75 **"Michael Jackson of autopsy":** Ibid., 92, 97.

76 **"speaking for the departed":** Jeanne Marie Laskas, "Bennet Omalu, Concussions, and the NFL: How One Doctor Changed Football Forever," *GQ,* September 14, 2009, www.gq.com/story/nfl-players-brain -dementia-study-memory-concussions.

76 **"became for him a calling":** Ibid.

77 **"with almost every *how*":** Friedrich Nietzsche, *The Twilight of the Idols* (New York: Macmillan, 1896), 98.

77 **"anxiety and depression":** Steve Taylor, "The Power of Purpose," *Psychology Today,* July 21, 2013, www.psychologytoday.com/blog/out -the-darkness/201307/the-power-purpose.

81 **"annihilate a man"**: Fyodor Dostoevsky, *The House of the Dead* (New York: Macmillan, 1915), 20.

82 **"curved-line, constant pursuit"**: Sarah Lewis, *The Rise* (New York: Simon & Schuster, 2014), 7–8.

83 **"literally names us"**: Al Gini, *My Job, My Self,* quoted in Todd Duncan, *Time Traps* (Nashville: Thomas Nelson, 2004), 18.

84 **"poets of our lives"**: Friedrich Nietzsche, *The Gay Science (The Joyful Wisdom)* (Overland Park, Kans.: Digireads, 2009), 112.

84 **"One sees clearly"**: Antoine de Saint-Exupéry, Richard Howard, trans., *The Little Prince* (New York: Mariner Books, 2000), 63.

88 **"I become hooked"**: Steven Pressfield, *The Authentic Swing* (n.p.: Black Irish Entertainment, 2013), 50.

90 **"your authentic swing"**: Jeremy Leven, *The Legend of Bagger Vance,* screenplay, directed by Robert Redford (2000; Los Angeles: Twentieth Century Fox).

95 **"we were relentless"**: Michka Assayas, *Bono: In Conversation* (New York: Riverhead Books, 2005), 62.

95 **"reflecting and amplifying"**: Natalie Goldberg, *Wild Mind* (New York: Bantam, 1990), 13.

Chapter 3: Keep Your Day Job

96 **"backfilling your life"**: Bob Goff, quoted in Kelsey Humphreys, "'How to Discover a Secretly Incredible Life in an Ordinary World'," *Success,* November 4, 2015, www.success.com/article/how-to-discover-a-secretly-incredible-life-in-an-ordinary-world.

97 **"wear one face"**: Nathaniel Hawthorne, *The Scarlet Letter* (New York: Dover, 1994), 147.

97 ***"end in madness"***: Edgar Lee Masters, "George Gray," *Spoon River Anthology* (New York: Dover, 1992), 30.

110 **"I love teaching"**: Thomas Bradshaw, "For Artists, Cheap Rent and Side Gigs Minimize Risk," *New York Times,* November 7, 2013, www

.nytimes.com/roomfordebate/2013/11/07/the-cost-of-being-an-artist
/for-artists-cheap-rent-and-side-gigs-minimize-risk.

111 **stands in contrast:** Clay Wirestone, "11 Celebrated Artists Who Didn't
Quit Their Day Jobs," *Mental Floss,* August 19, 2013, mentalfloss.com
/article/52293/11-celebrated-artists-who-didnt-quit-their-day-jobs;
Lydia Dishman, "10 Famous Creative Minds That Didn't Quit Their
Day Jobs," *Fast Company,* December 6, 2013, www.fastcompany.com
/3022985/how-to-be-a-success-at-everything/10-famous-creative
-minds-that-didnt-quit-their-day-jobs.

111 **used his daily walks:** Clay Wirestone, "11 Celebrated Artists Who
Didn't Quit Their Day Jobs," *Mental Floss,* August 19, 2013, www.men
talfloss.com/article/52293/11-celebrated-artists-who-didnt-quit
-their-day-jobs.

112 **"pretty dismal picture":** Juri Koll, "If You Want to Pursue the Arts
Don't Quit Your Day Job," *New York Times,* November 17, 2013, www
.nytimes.com/roomfordebate/2013/11/07/the-cost-of-being-an-artist
/if-you-want-to-pursue-the-arts-dont-quit-your-day-job.

112 **"get a day job":** AOL Jobs Staff, "6 Creatives Who Prove You Can
Hold a Day Job and Still Make Awesome Art," AOL Finance, October
6, 2014, www.aol.com/article/2014/10/06/gillian-robespierre-shane-jones
-day-jobs-career-advice/20967771.

113 **composer Philip Glass:** John O'Mahony, "When less means more,"
The Guardian, November 23, 2001, https://www.theguardian.com
/education/2001/nov/24/arts.highereducation1.

114 **"that having a job":** Richard Coad, "Traction #83: At Long Last, the Secret of Creativity Revealed," mdbcomm.com, http://www.mdbcomm.
com/blog/traction-83-at-long-last-the-secret-of-creativity-revealed.html.

115 **named lateral thinking:** De Bono's first book on the subject was *The
Use of Lateral Thinking* in 1967; however, his more well-known work is
the later, *Lateral Thinking: Creativity Step by Step* (New York: Harper &
Row, 1970).

115 **goal of lateral thinking:** Ibid.

116 **"sowing other seeds":** Glenn Llopis, *Earning Serendipity* (Austin, Tex.: Greenleaf, 2009), 10.

117 **rock band Loverboy:** Paul Dean, Mike Reno, and Matt Frenette, "Working for the Weekend," lyrics, Loverboy, on *Get Lucky*, produced by Dean and Bruce Fairbairn, Columbia Records, 1981.

118 **"seems to be doing both":** Lawrence Pearsall Jacks, *Education Through Recreation* (Washington, D.C.: McGrath Publishing Company and National Recreation and Park Association, 1960), 1–2.

Chapter 4: Embrace a Routine

119 **"sign of ambition":** W. H. Auden, quoted in Mason Currey, *Daily Rituals* (New York: Knopf, 2013), Kindle location 177.

122 **"discovering something new":** Mihaly Csikszentmihalyi, *Creativity* (New York: HarperPerennial, 2013), 108.

123 **"to face the unexpected":** Ibid., 108, 110, 109.

135 **"with iron regularity":** Oliver Burkeman, "Rise and shine: the daily routines of history's most creative minds," *The Guardian*, October 5, 2013, www.theguardian.com/science/2013/oct/05/daily-rituals-creative -minds-mason-currey.

136 **the more you repeat:** Daniel Coyle, *The Talent Code* (New York: Bantam, 2009), 5–6.

137 **"gray or blue suits":** Michael Lewis, "Obama's Way," *Vanity Fair*, September 11, 2012, www.vanityfair.com/news/2012/10/michael-lewis -profile-barack-obama.

140 **athlete like Mark Healey:** Thayer Walker, "Mark Healey Is the Greatest Athlete You've Never Heard Of," *Outside*, February 29, 2016, https:// www.outsideonline.com/2058516/mark-healey-greatest-athlete -youve-never-heard.

146 *Vogue* **editor in chief:** Huffington Post Healthy Living Editors, "The One Thing These Crazy Successful People Do Every Day," Shape.com,

www.shape.com/lifestyle/mind-and-body/one-thing-these-crazy
-successful-people-do-every-day.

146 **"Being in the mood to write":** Julia Cameron, *The Right to Write* (New York: Tarcher/Putnam, 1998), 33.

146 **perception to recognition:** C. S. Pierce, cited in Csikszentmihalyi, *Creativity*, 298.

147 **Ollestad grew up:** Norman Ollestad, *Crazy for the Storm* (New York: HarperCollins, 2009), 101–20.

Chapter 5: Defamiliarize the Ordinary

151 **"Genius is only":** creatingminds.org/quotes/seeing.htm.

152 **an apprentice cook:** Willard InterContinental, Washington, D.C., "Chef Antoine Westermann, Culinary Consultant, Café du Parc," washington.intercontinental.com/files/pdfs/press/Westerman.pdf.

153 **"so his creativity":** Le Coq Rico, "Chef Antoine Westermann," www
.lecoqriconyc.com/about.

153 **"offer something else":** Judy MacMahon, interview with Antoine Westermann, "Antoine Westermann Lives His Dream as a French Chef," *My French Life,* September 23, 2013, www.myfrenchlife
.org/2013/09/23/antoine-westermann-lives-his-dream-as-a-french
-chef.

156 **"That, and surprise":** Julia Cameron, *The Artist's Way* (New York: Tarcher/Putnam, 2002), 195.

159 **"*To see a World*":** William Blake, "Auguries of Innocence," *Poets of the English Language,* vol. 4 (New York: Viking Press, 1950).

160 **"that would be nice":** Adam Frank, "How to See the World in a Grain of Sand," *All Things Considered,* NPR, March 19, 2013, www.npr.org
/sections/13.7/2013/03/27/174647716/how-to-see-the-world-in
-a-grain-of-sand.

161 **"There is so much you can't learn":** *Jiro Dreams of Sushi,* directed by David Gelb (2012; New York: Magnolia Pictures).

NOTES

161 **"Most of us," he:** Steven Pressfield, *The War of Art* (n.p.: Black Irish Entertainment, 2012).

162 **fascinating creativity studies:** Carolyn Gregoire and Scott Barry Kaufman, "Creative People's Brains Really Do Work Differently," *Quartz*, January 4, 2016, qz.com/584850/creative-peoples-brains-really -do-work-differently.

167 **"two methods of attack":** Sun Tzu, *The Art of War* (Ballingslöv, Sweden: Chiron Academic Press, 2015), Kindle location 1098.

169 **"gracious uncertainty":** Oswald Chambers, *My Utmost for His Highest* (Grand Rapids, Mich.: Discovery House, 2012), Kindle location 1958.

172 **"the world breaks open":** Roy Williams, "The Price of Creativity," *Monday Morning Memo*, February 15, 2016, www.mondaymorning memo.com/newsletters/the-price-of-creativity.

173 **named Richard D. Grant:** Roy Williams, "5 Ways to Solve Problems Creatively," *Monday Morning Memo*, August 20, 2012, http://www .mondaymorningmemo.com/newsletters/5-ways-to-solve-problems -creatively.

174 **musician named Herb:** Roy Williams, "Herbert and the Bullfight," *Monday Morning Memo*, February 22, 2016, www.mondaymorning memo.com/newsletters/herbert-and-the-bullfight.

180 **secrets of Leonardo:** Kenneth Clark, quoted in Michael J. Gelb, *How to Think like Leonardo da Vinci* (New York: Random House, 2009), Kindle location 2972.

180 **"Leonardo's unparalleled creativity":** Ibid., Kindle location 2972.

181 **"took up his paintbrush":** Ibid., Kindle location 3034.

Chapter 6: Stay Foolish

182 **"I'm an artist":** Jann S. Wenner, "Lennon Remembers, Part One," *Rolling Stone*, January 21, 1971, http://www.rollingstone.com/music /news/lennon-remembers-part-one-19710121.

183 **"stupidest possible creative act":** Clay Shirky, *Cognitive Surplus* (New York: Penguin, 2010), 18–19.

183 **"lack formal training"**: Austin Kleon, *Show Your Work!* (New York: Workman, 2014), 16.

184 **"I learned about serif and sans serif"**: Valerie Strauss, "Steve Jobs Told Students: 'Stay Hungry. Stay Foolish,'" *Washington Post,* October 5, 2011, www.washingtonpost.com/blogs/answer-sheet/post/steve-jobs -told-students-stay-hungry-stay-foolish/2011/10/05/gIQA1qVjOL_blog .html.

186 **to relearn something:** Matt Fitzgerald, *How Bad Do You Want It?* (Boulder, Colo.: Velopress, 2015), 105.

189 **"Willie Stewart discovered"**: Ibid., 92, 101, 107.

194 **"When someone has the insight"**: Peter Sims, *Little Bets* (New York: Simon & Schuster, 2013), 9.

195 **"might be great"**: Ibid., 10–11.

197 **NASA's Jet Propulsion Laboratory:** Kelly Dickerson, "There's a Crazy True Story About NASA Mentioned in 'The Martian,'" *Tech Insider,* October 7, 2015, www.techinsider.io/nasa-jpl-founding-story -the-martian-2015-10.

198 **125 NASA missions:** Jet Propulsion Laboratory, California Institute of Techonology, "History & Archives," www.jpl.nasa.gov/about/history.php.

198 **"Everyone has a plan"**: Mike Tyson, in Mike Bernadino, "Mike Tyson Explains One of His Most Famous Quotes," *Sun Sentinel,* November 9, 2012, articles.sun-sentinel.com/2012-11-09/sports/sfl-mike-tyson-ex plains-one-of-his-most-famous-quotes-20121109_1_mike-tyson -undisputed-truth-famous-quotes.

Chapter 7: Fall in Love

203 **"the object it loves"**: C. G. Jung, *The Collected Works of C. G. Jung, Vol. 6: Psychological Types* (Princeton, N. J.: Princeton University Press, 1971), Kindle location 2512.

203 **"Even on her deathbed"**: Barbara Goldsmith, *Obsessive Genius: The Inner World of Marie Curie,* Great Discoveries series (New York: Norton, 2005), 215.

205 **"he alone loves"**: Annie Dillard, *The Writing Life* (New York: Harper-Perennial, 1990), 67.

206 **"6,000 plant species"**: "Wade Davis: The Explorer's Explorer," *Time: Modern Explorers,* July 2015, 90.

206 **photographer Robbie Shone:** "Robbie Shone: Illuminating the Darkness," ibid., 68.

206 **"it's like going home"**: Sylvia Earle, quoted in Bryan Walsh: "Code Blue," ibid., 32.

206 **"Most of the days"**: John Branch, "Abduction. Lost Finger. Now, a Rock Climber's Tallest Hurdle," *New York Times*, January 7, 2015, www.nytimes.com/2015/01/08/sports/on-el-capitan-dawn-wall-in-yosemite-and-beyond-climber-tommy-caldwells-drive-pushes-him-toward-the-impossible.html?_r=0.

207 **the climbers spoke:** "I Would Love for This to Open People's Minds," *New York Times*, January 14, 2015, www.nytimes.com/2015/01/15/sports/el-capitans-dawn-wall-climbers-reach-top.html.

208 **"Earlier times may not"**: Susan Neiman in *Moral Clarity,* quoted in Jon Krakauer, *Where Men Win Glory* (New York: Anchor Books, 2010), 1.

211 **"Love people and lift them up"**: Hong Thaimee, conversation with the author, April 29, 2016.

212 **"As Jesus and his disciples"**: Luke 10:38–42 (New International Version).

213 **"making eggs at 6:30"**: Glenn Rifkin, "Helping Homeless Artists Turn Around Their Fortunes," *New York Times*, February 17, 2016, www.nytimes.com/2016/02/18/business/smallbusiness/homeless-artists-gallery-artlifting.html?_r=0.

215 **"flow the springs of life"**: Proverbs 4:23 (New American Standard Bible).

216 **"It's a mess"**: Andrew Tate, "5 Reasons Creative Geniuses Like Einstein, Twain and Zuckerberg Had Messy Desks—And Why You Should Too," *Canva,* May 29, 2015, designschool.canva.com/blog/creative-desks.

INDEX